A BRIEF HISTORY of LOS ALAMITOS & ROSSMOOR

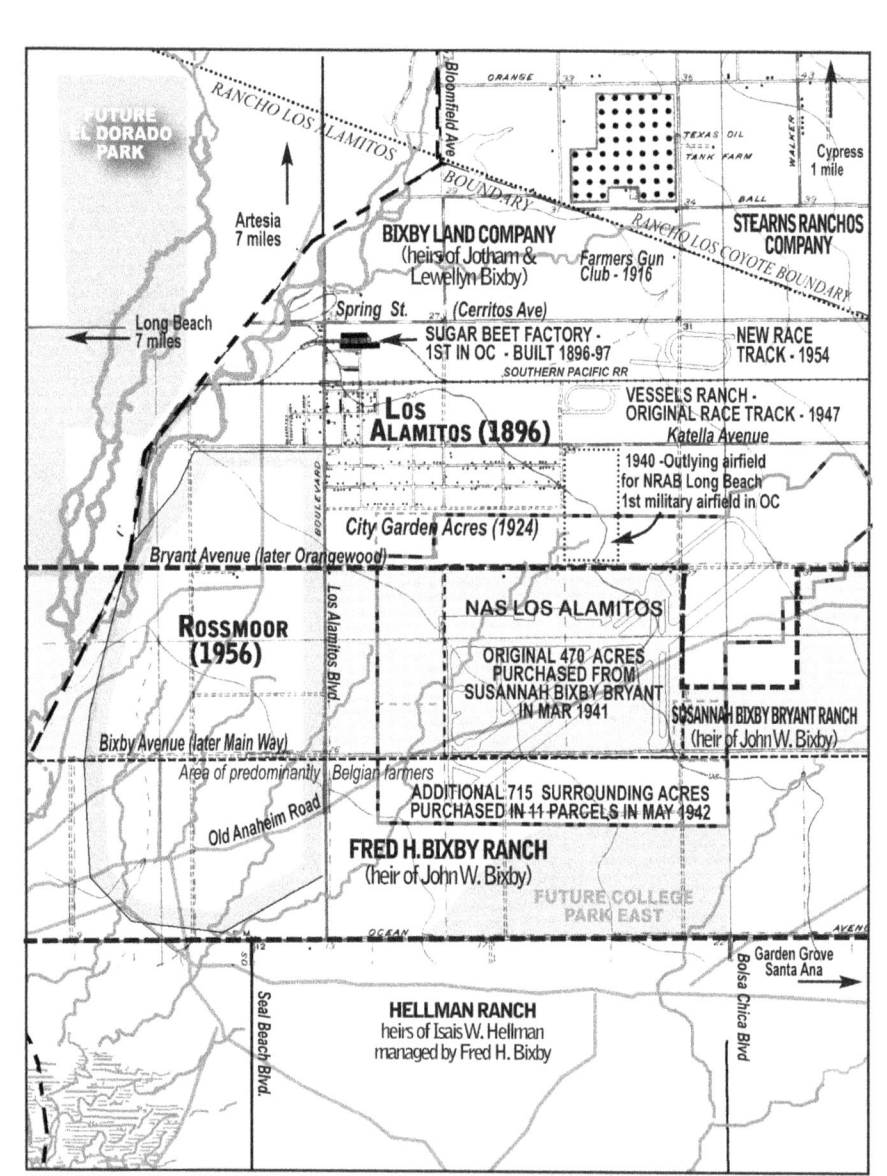

HISTORICAL LOS ALAMITOS — Pre-1955 newspapers usually referred to Los Alamitos as that part of Orange County within the Rancho Los Alamitos and north of Westminster Blvd. and west of Hansen (Golden West) Ave. This obviously included Rossmoor and also large parts of what are now Seal Beach, Cypress and Garden Grove.

A BRIEF HISTORY *of*
LOS ALAMITOS & ROSSMOOR

LARRY STRAWTHER

Published by The History Press
Charleston, SC 29403
www.historypress.net

Copyright © 2012 by Larry Strawther
All rights reserved

Front cover, top: Children lining up to ring the bell at the opening of the 1917 sugar beet campaign. *Bottom*: Watercolor of Main Street, circa 1919, by local artist John Partridge. *Images courtesy of the Los Alamitos Museum.*

First published 2012
Second printing 2013
Third printing 2013

ISBN 978.1.5402.0779.1

Library of Congress CIP data applied for

Notice: The information in this book is true and complete to the best of our knowledge. It is offered without guarantee on the part of the author or The History Press. The author and The History Press disclaim all liability in connection with the use of this book.

All rights reserved. No part of this book may be reproduced or transmitted in any form whatsoever without prior written permission from the publisher except in the case of brief quotations embodied in critical articles and reviews.

To my wonderful wife, Nancy, and my always interesting children, Megan, Michael and Mallory, for putting up with me—and my twenty-three binders of notes, photocopies, old articles and photos that sometimes filled bookcases but more often than not were spread out on my desk or on the floor behind me.

To John W. Bixby, Frank Capitain and Ross Cortese, for having a vision and the passion and persistence to make it happen and, in the process, helping to create a great place to live and raise a family.

CONTENTS

Preface	9
1. The Land, the Rivers and the First Inhabitants	13
2. Abel Stearns and Rancho Days	19
3. The Bixbys: An Empire of Sheep	25
4. The Bixbys: Town Building	32
5. The Clarks, Sugar and a New Town	39
6. Railroads, Immigrants and Fred Bixby	54
7. Oil, Sugar Blues, Horse Meat and Earthquakes	74
8. The Base	95
9. After the War: The Racetrack and Small Town, USA	107
10. Ross Cortese and Rossmoor	128
11. Cityhood for Los Al	140
Epilogue	149
Sources	151
About the Author	157

PREFACE

In September 2012, the large nationwide real estate firm Coldwell Banker released a study of more than eleven thousand communities that ranked Rossmoor as the number one suburban community in California and number nine in the nation. The rankings were based on a number of factors, including traffic conditions, local school quality and proximity to amenities such as gas stations, ATMs and grocery stores.

For the record, the Rossmoor being ranked was in Southern California (near Long Beach), not to be confused with the Rossmoor in Northern California, which, although developed by the same builder, is a seniors'/retirement community. On the contrary, the southern Rossmoor is full of kids, which makes its school and sports leagues even more fun to watch.

While its number one ranking is well deserved, in all fairness, Rossmoor needs to share this achievement with its next-door neighbors: northern Seal Beach and, to a much greater extent, Los Alamitos. Rossmoor couldn't exist without Los Alamitos, nor could Los Alamitos exist as it is today without Rossmoor. The communities share schools, churches, commerce, youth sports leagues, social organizations, a fire department and a library system—almost everything that makes up a community except city council members, a police department and a couple narrow-minded curmudgeons.

Although I didn't grow up in the Los Alamitos–Rossmoor area, my wife did, which is why we moved to Rossmoor in 1997. Since then, I have

Preface

grown to really like this community. It's a great place to live—often in spite of itself.

We do get a little too passionate about local politics and local youth sports and our schools. But we rarely get passionate about our history, which is a shame because we have an interesting story to tell. Many important events and achievements have happened here and have had an impact on the surrounding communities more than they know.

But most of these events have been accomplished in relative anonymity or lost in confusion—which is not too surprising for a community where the Los Alamitos Racetrack is in Cypress and the Los Alamitos–Rossmoor Library is in Seal Beach, as is the Rossmoor Center (which is even more confusing now after having been renamed The Shops at Rossmoor/Seal Beach).

Historical Los Alamitos is much larger than the present city. For our purposes, its territory includes Los Alamitos and Rossmoor and adjacent parts of Seal Beach, Cypress and Garden Grove. It is closely intertwined with the development of Long Beach and Lakewood. A strong argument can be made that the history of this area is also a microcosm of western United States history, touching on Native Americans, Spanish and Mexican settlement, the California gold rush, westward expansion, the Civil War, the growth of the railroads, the age of capitalism and robber barons, the growth of aviation and aerospace, petroleum, early motion pictures, World War II, the growth of suburbia and walled communities, not to mention modern real estate marketing and many other aspects.

Even accounting for the inevitable local exaggeration and embroidery, elements of all of the above did take place here, although most of the main players usually resided elsewhere.

Geography and climate played major roles. The low and flat terrain and frequent floods delayed significant subdivision until well into the twentieth century, thus making it desirable for the military bases, which provided yet another natural barrier that ensured isolation.

Finally, the river channels were lined with concrete and the floods tamed, which quickly led to Ross Cortese's development of Rossmoor—one of Southern California's largest real estate developments. By 1961, the original

Preface

Rossmoor had over thirteen thousand residents. In comparison, Los Alamitos had four thousand and Seal Beach, six thousand.

While the community's story continued, our story ends at the end of 1960, a natural break marking the end of the historic past and the beginning of the present and future.

Obviously, this story couldn't have been told without the input of a lot of people. Time and space doesn't allow me to name them all, but I'd especially like to thank longtime area residents Margrit Kendrick, Marilynn Poe, Leon Sjostrom, Jim Bell Jr. and Sherry Campbell Poe. I'd also like to thank Pamela Seagar and the staff at the Rancho Los Alamitos Museum, Steve Iverson at Rancho Los Cerritos and the folks at the California, Anaheim and Long Beach Historical Societies

There is probably more information in this book about Los Alamitos and Rossmoor than anybody really wants to know, but I figured that since nobody had thoroughly covered the subject before, why not try to throw as much mud as possible against the wall and see what sticks.

Still this work doesn't tell the whole story, but hopefully it will leave you understanding a little bit better how we got where we are and why we're heading in the direction we're traveling. And perhaps you can also take solace in the knowledge that if we haven't hurt ourselves yet, we probably won't in the future.

1
THE LAND, THE RIVERS AND THE FIRST INHABITANTS

The land around Los Alamitos and Rossmoor is flat. The highest natural point, on the Los Alamitos Air Base, is just shy of thirty-six feet above sea level, with the lowest point, west of Hopkinson School in Rossmoor, at just under ten feet—a drop of only twenty-five feet over four miles. Even our highest natural point is lower than the tops of the levee walls that contain Coyote Creek and the San Gabriel River.

Before those levees were built, we were frequently flooded when heavy rains carried water from the San Gabriel Mountains. Geologically speaking, the San Gabriels are young, still rising as rapidly as any range in the world. Riddled with faults, they crumble easily and rapidly in the face of Pacific Ocean storms but still build up faster than they disintegrate.

Most storms blowing in from the Pacific Ocean stall at least momentarily at the San Gabriels, sometimes releasing some of the most concentrated precipitation ever recorded in the nation—one 1943 storm dumped twenty-six inches on Hoegee's Camp in a twenty-four-hour period. As the mountain soils become saturated, massive debris of boulders, gravel, sand and silt flow off the mountains and into canyon streams, which are just starting their journey toward the ocean. Most of the water does not make it.

In the level flood plains of the San Gabriel Valley and Los Angeles basin, the crumbly rocks settled into the gravelly soil—in some places thirty thousand feet (or six miles) deep. Gravity induced most of the water to sink into the large three-hundred-square-mile aquifer, an underground river that slowly makes its way through the slanted layers of sediment that descend to the ocean.

After flowing through the gap in the Puente Hills—the Paso de Bartolo (now the Whittier Narrows)—the water of the San Gabriel burst into the main Los Angeles basin. On the surface, it forged and re-forged channels on a whim. Over millions of years, it has sometimes sent its water down the Rio Hondo channel to merge with the Los Angeles River or sometimes south to join up with Coyote Creek, often doing both. In times of extremely great rainfall, Coyote Creek and the San Gabriel, Los Angeles and Santa Ana Rivers would spread out and join up in one vast sheet of water fifteen miles wide, at times making the country impassable for weeks.

But in normal years, most of the San Gabriel's water disappeared into the alluvial sediments. The little that stayed above ground meandered, leaving trails that, from the air, looked like twisted braids over the flat terrain, leaving a rich fertile silt and loam in its wake.

Most of the San Gabriel River and Coyote Creek water disappeared into the alluvial soils and the aquifer beneath the Los Angeles basin. But as both streams passed Los Alamitos and hit the dam that is the Newport-Inglewood fault, the waters backed up very close to the surface, creating heavily wooded thickets and brush alongside the creek and river. Early settlers said the thickets were home to bear, deer and other wildlife.

The Land, the Rivers and the First Inhabitants

Near the ocean, these underground waters encountered a natural dam of clay and rock, a fault line running from Newport Beach to Inglewood. Above ground, it is a string of highlands: the Bolsa Chica Bluffs, "The Hill" in Seal Beach, Bixby Hill, Signal Hill, Dominguez Hills, Baldwin Hills and Cheviot Hills.

Eventually, the rivers wore down and created four gaps through this natural barrier: by Newport Bay, Anaheim Bay, Alamitos Bay and Wilmington. Floodwaters could now reach the ocean, but tides could also bring some salt water inland.

Except for Bixby Hill and Signal Hill, much of Southeast Long Beach and far west Orange County was tidal wetlands. Portions of Anaheim Bay—marshy sloughs—reached up beyond the present San Diego Freeway into Rossmoor, near Hopkinson School and by the Old Ranch Town Center, forming lakes, ponds and marshes. Historical ecologists state that below the confluence of Coyote Creek and the San Gabriel River, the streams would sometimes split their flow, sending some into Anaheim Bay and some into Alamitos Bay. Even on the slightly higher land, the high-water table made much of present Los Alamitos, especially the part west of Bloomfield, into a large alkali meadow that reached as far north as Ball Road.

The wetlands were natural cleaning agents. The sun's ultraviolet light helped kill viruses, while the soil filtered out bacteria. Above the wetlands, groves of shrub, willows and cottonwoods interspersed with marsh in the creek bottoms. Fish and smaller mammals thrived in the wetlands, which in turn attracted bigger animals. Early settlers said the thickets were home to bear, deer and other wildlife.

The area's climate and abundant food supply of fish and game no doubt attracted the earliest human settlers—around 2,500 years ago or 6,000 years ago, depending on which expert you believe. Many assume these first settlers in California were of Hokan linguistic stock. But between 500 BC and AD 1200, natives of Shoshone linguistic stock made their way from the Great Basin of Utah and Nevada to the Southern California coast. This intrusion is called the Shoshonean Wedge. The early Spanish called the indigenous population around here *Gabrielino* because of the proximity to the Mission San Gabriel.

But the Native Americans called themselves the Puvu, the Pubu, the Puvitsi and, most often, the Tongva.

The Tongva built between fifty and one hundred villages in the Greater Los Angeles and Northern Orange County area: in the San Fernando, San Gabriel and Santa Ana Valleys, in the Los Angeles Basin and on the Palos Verdes peninsula. They left us with many familiar names—Pacoima, Cahuenga, Tujunga, Topanga, Azusa and Cucamonga. The villages of Suvangna and Awingna were near Coyote Hills Golf Course. Sejat (Village of the Bees) was at the Whittier Narrows, and Tibahangna lay near the Los Angeles River on the property of Rancho Los Cerritos. Remains indicating other villages have been found in San Pedro, Irvine, the Bolsa Chica bluffs and Seal Beach's Marina Hill.

There is evidence of many settlements around the San Gabriel estuary. One of the largest, Puvungva, was on Bixby Hill, by Cal State Long Beach, where the underground dam forced water up into a reliable, natural spring of fresh water for the area's inhabitants. Evidence of these early inhabitants is all around the hill—near Whaley Park (Bellflower and Atherton), by Studebaker and Anaheim and another in El Dorado Park, north of its present confluence with Coyote Creek.

Tongva society included extensive trade; technological achievements (artistically advanced knives and bowls, baskets woven so tight they could hold water and very seaworthy plank canoes); formalized birth, rite-of-passage and death traditions; and a belief in a supreme being, Chingchinich.

There was a sizable Tongva population in Southern California—estimates range from five to fifteen thousand—when Juan Rodriguez Cabrillo, a Portuguese navigator sailing under the Spanish flag, sailed into San Pedro Bay in 1542. Cabrillo noted the smoke from many villages, calling it the "Bay of Smokes."

Although Cabrillo claimed California for the king of Spain, the area was left alone by the Spanish conquerors for over two hundred years, until other European powers showed interest in the area. Most concerning were the Russians, who had created a very profitable fur trade in the Pacific Northwest and established a post north of San Francisco Bay.

The Land, the Rivers and the First Inhabitants

To thwart Russian colonization, the Spaniards planned four coordinated expeditions to California—two by sea, two by land. In 1769, Father Junipero Serra established Mission San Diego, the first of twenty-one over the next fifty-four years, to bring the Spanish gift of Catholicism to the California natives—and, incidentally, to secure the land for the Spanish crown. In mid-July 1769, a second land expedition under Don Gaspar de Portola set out north in search of Monterey Bay after leaving about half its force of 130 men back in San Diego.

Portola's company of friars, leather-jacketed soldiers, muleteers, servants and Indian neophytes made their way along a trail that roughly followed what is now Interstate 5. They named the range of mountains to their east for the Feast Day of St. Ann. After two weeks, they camped along a river across from a sizable native village near present Angels Stadium. That day, they experienced two earthquakes. Father Juan Crespi named the river for Jesus and the quakes (*Nombre Dulce de Jesus de los Temblores*), but the soldiers—who included Captain Pedro Fages (Portola's second in command), Corporal Manuel Nieto, and Privates Jose María Verdugo and Juan Jose Domínguez—thought the river's origins were in the nearby mountains and called it simply the Santa Ana River. As usual, simplicity won the day. The company continued their trek north, passing through the Coyote Hills, which provided an excellent view of the land toward Palos Verdes and Signal Hill. Fages, Nieto and the others would remember the good grazing land in the Los Angeles basin.

Fages eventually became governor and Nieto was assigned to the garrison at San Diego. In 1784, with retirement approaching, he petitioned his former commander for the right to graze his cattle on some of the good land around the Santa Ana River. Fages granted him, as well as Verdugo and Dominguez, the first provisional ranchos in California. (Technically, they were little more than grazing permits. The king of Spain still owned the land.) The Nieto "grant" was by far the largest—300,000 acres—and it originally included land much closer to the pueblo at Los Angeles. But to resolve issues with the priests at San Gabriel, Fages made some adjustments. The final boundaries of Nieto's grant eventually were defined as being between the Santa Ana and San Gabriel Rivers (which then emptied where the Los Angeles River now empties) and on the north from the main road leading to Mission San Gabriel south to the ocean. Although reduced to 167,000 acres, it was still the largest grant ever made by the Spanish or Mexican governments in California.

Nieto settled on that portion of his land near Downey, along the main road that became known as El Camino Real. When he died in 1804, the land passed to his widow. Their oldest son, Juan Jose, reportedly built an adobe on the southern edge of their land by the Puvungva Spring, where the Tongva villages had by now been abandoned because of disease, assimilation into the Spanish friars' community at the San Gabriel or, for a smaller number, an escape from the Spanish friars' influence by moving into the "backcountry."

Another former soldier, Patricio Ontiveros, saw the potential of the land near the spring and the *alamitos* (the little cottonwoods) around it. He petitioned Governor Figueroa for it, saying it had been vacated by Nieto. No doubt concerned, Juan Jose Nieto asked Figueroa for a confirmation of his father's grant from the new Mexican government and requested a division of the land among Manuel's heirs. Juan Jose hired a young Yankee immigrant named Abel Stearns to make a *diseño*, a survey of the land. In June 1833, Figueroa granted the separation of the vast grant into five separate ranchos: Las Bolsa, Los Cerritos, Los Coyotes, Santa Gertrudes and Los Alamitos. Perhaps not so coincidentally, within a year Juan Jose sold the governor the Alamitos rancho at a very cheap price.

Figueroa formed a company, the *Compania Agriculturia*, to stock and manage the land, but his untimely death in 1835 would end that enterprise. But the quality of the land had not escaped the notice of the Yankee who had surveyed Juan Jose's diseño. And Abel Stearns understood the value of land as well as any man in California.

2
ABEL STEARNS AND RANCHO DAYS

Abel Stearns's name appears with "monotonous regularity" in any history of Southern California from 1830 to 1870. Born in Massachusetts in 1798 and orphaned at an early age, Stearns went to sea at age twelve and learned the South American and China trade before making his way to the newly independent republic of Mexico. His stay there was brief, but he formed good relationships with important British merchants, became a Mexican citizen and obtained from the government a shadowy concession to an immense tract of land somewhere in the California interior.

Stearns sailed to Monterey in 1829 and then migrated to Los Angeles, where he established himself as a merchant, bartering groceries, liquors and dry goods for the hides and tallow from the surrounding ranchos. He also purchased furs from the growing number of American trappers coming to California on the heels of Jedediah Smith and others.

To better deal with seafaring American merchants, Stearns established a warehouse in San Pedro and gained control of much of the southern California trade, becoming wealthy and influential in the process. So it wasn't by chance that Juan Nieto enlisted Stearns's support to prepare his diseño in opposition to Patricio Ontivero's request for the Puvungva land. And if he wasn't already familiar with the property, Stearns's survey would inevitably make him very familiar with its qualities.

A Brief History of Los Alamitos and Rossmoor

Abel Stearns was one of California's most influential merchants from 1830 to 1870. He bought the Alamitos in 1844, the first in a series of acquisitions that would make him the largest landowner in California. The drought of the 1860s forced him to the brink of financial ruin, and he lost the Alamitos to San Francisco moneylender Michael Reese. But friends rallied to preserve the rest of his lands, which were put up for sale as the Stearns Ranchos in 1867. The property includes the Orange County land surrounding the Rancho Los Alamitos (Cypress, West Anaheim, Buena Park, Fullerton, Garden Grove, Westminster and Huntington Beach).

With his work for Nieto and its success, Stearns's reputation and influence continued to grow—first through his friendship with the influential Don Juan Bandini and then through his 1839 marriage to the don's daughter, Arcadia. Their new home in Los Angeles, El Palacio, at the corner of what are now Main and Arcadia Streets, became a center for pueblo society for the next thirty years.

In 1835, Governor Figueroa died, and without his leadership (and governmental influence), his *Compania Agriculturia* faltered and was dissolved. Legalities and distance to Mexico delayed matters, but finally the Alamitos was put on the market. In 1840, just a year after his marriage, Stearns purchased the rancho, paying around $6,000 for its "900 cattle, nearly 1,000 sheep & 240 horses," as well as "6 sq. leagues of land, a small house & a few other triflings worth some $200."

The California gold rush and the arriving miners' appetite for beef ushered in a spectacular boom for cattle. Stearns built up the largest land and cattle empire in Southern California. His knowledge of Southern

Abel Stearns and Rancho Days

California business affairs enabled him to add one financially troubled ranch after another to his holdings. Stearns soon acquired the 11,000-acre rancho La Laguna, a substantial interest in Rancho Las Bolsas, and soon after the choice 6,800-acre La Bolsa Chica, a fractional interest in the Rancho Temescal (near Corona), the Rancho Los Coyotes and parts of the Ranchos San Juan Cajon de Santa Ana, Santiago de Santa Ana and La Jurupa.

All this fertile soil provided an ideal base for Stearns and his growing herds of cattle, which roamed the valleys, plains and rolling hills—often covered with yellow mustard and higher than a man's head.

The thickset stalks made an ideal hiding place for cattle, and local rancheros held special roundups to gather and separate the cattle. In 1852, C.H. Brinley, manager of the Los Alamitos, wrote to Stearns to tell him of a "run of two or three days planned at the Nietos. The Temples, Manuel Dominguez and the Coyotes will be there sure, and most likely a sufficient number of people will be brought together to effect some good."

Brinley is a colorful yet rarely mentioned character in the Los Alamitos saga. Like Stearns, he was a native of Massachusetts. He spent time in the China trade, lived in Canton and, in 1851, he ended up on the executive committee of the San Francisco Committee of Vigilance, along with some of San Francisco's most prominent leaders. Shortly after, Brinley showed up as major-domo on Stearns's Rancho Los Alamitos, where he was a no-nonsense manager.

He had no problem firing family or friends who he felt were lazy. Nor did he have any qualms over using the virtual slave labor of Native Americans. In 1852, he wrote to Stearns to "deputize someone to attend the auction that usually takes place at the prison on Mondays and buy me five or six Indians." Nor was he intimidated by rank or social position. He flatly accused Stearns's well-regarded neighbor, Jose Sepulveda, of selling 150 branded cattle belonging to Stearns.

Cattle were not the only stock to forage on the Alamitos and other lands owned by Stearns. As early as 1854, he was leasing out portions of the Alamitos to Basque sheepherders, most of whom emigrated during the gold rush from Argentina and Chile. For payment, Stearns charged a share of the offspring.

A Brief History of Los Alamitos and Rossmoor

By 1862, Stearns had acquired or controlled over 200,000 acres of the choicest land in Los Angeles and San Bernardino Counties and was the most important landowner in Southern California. He held numerous public offices and identified himself with nearly every charitable or civic enterprise undertaken in Los Angeles. But he also invested in several unprofitable mining ventures, opened a flour mill in Los Angeles and, in 1858, even as the cattle boom drew to an end, erected the celebrated Arcadia Building in Los Angeles, which stood at the southwest corner of Arcadia and Los Angeles Streets. The two-story, well-equipped brick building was reputed to be the largest business block south of San Francisco. It contained eight stores, returned from $600 to $800 a month in rentals and represented an investment of about $85,000.

But before he could finish the building, Stearns ran short on money. A drop in cattle prices and taxes stretched his finances. To finish construction, he borrowed $20,000, with an interest rate at 1½ percent per month, from a San Francisco financier, Michael Reis (usually now spelled Reese). Stearns used the Alamitos as security.

As the Civil War began, Stearns found himself land and cattle rich but very cash poor. Things did not improve. Unprecedented rains and flooding throughout California in December 1861 and January 1862 created a huge inland sea, deep enough in some places to cover the tops of telegraph poles. Thousands of cattle drowned, including many on the Alamitos. Then spring's abundant supply of grass added greatly to the fatness of the remaining herds, causing a glut on the beef market that caused cattle prices to drop to pre–gold rush era.

The floods were followed by an unparalleled two-year drought, which along with a plague of grasshoppers stripped what little vegetation remained. With no grass to feed on, cattle began dying all over the Southern California ranchos. The editor of the *Southern News* reported, "The cattle of Los Angeles County are dying so fast in many places for want of food…Thousands of carcasses strew the plains in all directions, a short distance from this city…famine has done its work and nothing can now save what few cattle remain on the desert California ranches."

After all this Stearns' obligations far exceeded his income, and a number of his notes were "long overdue."

Abel Stearns and Rancho Days

In February 1865, a Los Angeles court issued a decree of sale against the Rancho Los Alamitos. Stearns obtained a year's extension on the note but failed to raise the necessary funds. In 1866, the land of the "Little Cottonwoods" defaulted into the hands of Reese.

Before he lost other properties, Stearns was rescued by a longtime friend and business associate, Alfred Robinson, who interested a group of San Francisco investors in a plan to subdivide and sell Stearns's holdings in Southern California. This group is commonly called the Robinson Trust and included Robinson, Sam Brannan, Edward F. Northam, Charles B. Polhemus and Edward Martin, as well as Stearns. The latter conveyed all his remaining ranchos (except La Laguna) in Los Angeles and San Bernardino Counties to the syndicate, who in turn paid him a dollar and half per acre once the land was sold. The agreement involved 177,796 acres—nearly 278 square miles—of fertile, adaptable land.

The trust, under the name of the Los Angeles and San Bernardino Land Company, distributed thousands of maps of the Stearns ranchos throughout the United States and Europe. Agents flooded the East with literature describing the incomparable climate and agricultural advantages of Southern California and employed well-known lecturers and writers to advertise the many attractions, real and imagined, of the land. Every time a steamship left San Francisco for Los Angeles, trust agents were on board to describe the Stearns land. Twenty- and fifty-acre plots sold for five to thirteen dollars an acre.

Disregarding the old Spanish and Mexican rancho boundary lines, the Trust's surveyors used the U.S. federal government's standard range-tract grid system. Rancho lands were divided into one-mile-square tracts of 640 acres and then subdivided into half-mile squares of 160 acres. (This explains why most major roads in Orange County now occur every half mile—along the section boundary lines.) Most tracts, or sections, were further subdivided into farms containing from 20 to 160 acres.

The trust also attached itself to the California Immigrant Union, a booster organization formed by large landholders to recruit people to move to California.

Relations grew sour between the trust and Stearns, who had been his own master far too long. Despite the agreement, Stearns still leased out land on the ranchos La Habra, Los Coyotes and San Juan Canon de Santa Ana to sheep men. Even his longtime friend Alfred Robinson charged Stearns with "carelessness and matters of grave importance, of fussing about horses" and pasturing them on company land, placing obstacles in the way of sale of the land.

But the friction would not impede the success of the trust. New settlement and diversified agriculture—and the success of the Anaheim colony—was creating an insatiable demand for homes and small farms, and the Stearns Ranchos and Trust had tens of thousands of acres.

By 1870, the syndicate had sold more than twenty thousand acres, and Stearns, fully recovered from the financial debacle of the 1860s, was on the eve of again amassing one of the greatest California fortunes when he was stricken with a sudden illness while on a business trip to San Francisco. He died there on August 23, 1871.

3
THE BIXBYS: AN EMPIRE OF SHEEP

The next characters to take center stage in our story were three men from Maine: Lewellyn Bixby and his cousins, Benjamin and Thomas Flint.

In February 1849, just weeks after President Zachary Polk announced the discovery of gold in California, Benjamin Flint left Maine for a four-month journey through the Isthmus of Panama to San Francisco (a passenger on the same ship as Collis Huntington and James Irvine) and then to the mining town of Volcano, where it was said one miner took out $8,000 worth of gold in a few days.

Spurred by such reports, younger brother Thomas Flint and two Bixby cousins, Amasa Jr. and Lewellyn, joined Ben in California in 1851, followed in 1852 by two more Bixby brothers, Jotham and Marcellus, and two Bixby cousins. Eventually, seven of Lewellyn's brothers, his two sisters and his father-in-law would migrate to California.

The Maine men quickly learned that supplying the growing population of Volcano provided more financial opportunities than mining in freezing streams. Lewellyn Bixby started working in a butcher shop, which he later bought in partnership with the Flints. Thomas Flint built a hotel, and Jotham and Marcellus operated a small farm and sold their harvests to the miners.

A Brief History of Los Alamitos and Rossmoor

While Southern California ranchers like Abel Stearns could supply all the beef, there were still opportunities for sheep. Mutton could be sold at twenty dollars per head, wool could be utilized and California's vast unsettled acreage created a low cost of pasturage.

Benjamin, Thomas and Lewellyn pooled $5,000 to return east and purchase sheep and cattle to bring back to California. Their one-year journey was detailed in Thomas's quite thorough diary.

They set out on Christmas 1852. After a month of travel back through Panama to Maine, and another month of visiting, they boarded a train west. In Terre Haute, Indiana, where the tracks ended, the three formed the partnership of Flint, Bixby & Company and then spent the next two months scouring southern Indiana and Illinois, buying sheep. In May, they sheared their new flock of two thousand and sold the wool for $1,570.64. By now, the warmer temperatures

In 1850, Dr. Thomas Flint (right) and cousin Lewellyn Bixby (left) joined Flint's brother Benjamin in California during the Gold Rush. The Flints and Bixby made more money by supplying the miners than looking for gold themselves. They returned to Maine in late 1852. After visiting their family, they took a train to Terre Haute, Indiana, where in 1853 they formed Flint, Bixby & Company and spent the next few months buying over two thousand sheep, which they then drove to California and started a business.

The Bixbys: An Empire of Sheep

had melted the snow and dried and hardened the ground enough for the company of men, sheep, oxen, cows, horses and wagons to start their 2,000 mile trek west, paralleling the Oregon and Mormon Trails across the plains.

Going at a sheep's pace, Lewellyn found it pleasanter to walk. They encountered problems with Indians—including the murder of one of their crew while standing guard. Once, a half dozen Indians bounded out of the brush and commenced to pillage the wagons until a teamster's wife went after their hands with a hatchet as they reached for belongings in her wagon. The Indians then revealed a certificate in immaculate penmanship stating that they were good Indians and would hopefully be treated well. Flint said they gave them hard tack and a sheep that was lame.

Shortly after, the party overtook a desolate train of Mormon emigrants from England who had been robbed of their provisions by these "Good Indians." The Yankee sheep men gave them—and other needy Mormon emigrants along the way—sufficient food to carry them to their New Zion destination in the Salt Lake Valley.

In August, hurricane-like winds buffeted them with sand for fifteen minutes. Two days later, "the air was full of grasshoppers, partially obscuring the sun." But on "delightful mornings," they "breakfasted on tea, coffee, bacon, warm bread, pepper sauce and pickles" and "beans cooked in the ground, a hole heated and filled in with coals." They rose about 4:00 a.m. every morning and hit the trail before it got too warm.

On August 13, they crossed the Continental Divide at South Pass and continued through the Rocky Mountains. Two weeks later, they entered the Salt Lake Valley, where non-Mormons, especially those from Illinois and Missouri where Mormons had been run out of the states, were encouraged to move on or pay exorbitant fines for trumped-up charges. But the Flint-Bixby party, because of their generosity and assistance to the migrating Saints, were "kindly received and treated wherever we went."

They spent almost three weeks in "Brigham's Kingdom," recuperating and replenishing their supplies, then set out for California via the southern route—the old Spanish Trail that parallels much of modern Interstate 15.

A day ahead of the Flint-Bixby train was Colonel William Welles Hollister, driving six thousand sheep from Ohio to California. The two parties stayed close, cooperating in overcoming difficulties and defending against the Indians and, on occasion, the Mormons and the threat of their zealous Avenging Angels.

Entering Nevada, they left Indian problems behind but still had to rescue cattle from muddy riverbeds and travel at night during long stretches without water, such as near Las Vegas Springs and the Mojave Desert. Finally, on New Year's Day, they passed over the Cajon Pass near San Bernardino and would end up wintering the herd near present-day Pasadena before continuing north in March.

With the money from their first sale of wool and mutton, the new company partnered with William Hollister to buy the Rancho San Justo south of San Jose. Throughout the 1850s, Flint-Bixby increased their flocks and expanded their holdings. In 1854, the total wool clip for California was less than 200,000 pounds. A decade later, the clip was thirty times that.

In 1857, both Flints married women from New England. Two years later, in Skowhegan, Maine, Lewellyn married Sarah Hathaway, one of five daughters of a well-known Congregationalist pastor. Lewellyn's brother Jotham would marry Sarah's sister Margaret in 1862. When Sarah died, Lewellyn married another Hathaway sister, Mary.

During the Civil War, the Union blockade of Southern cotton created a demand for wool. As wool prices soared, so did the Flint-Bixby fortunes.

The drought of 1862–64, which almost ruined Stearns, also caused problems for Flint-Bixby, but the financial problems for cattle ranchers were generally opportunities for the sheep men.

Beginning in 1864, Flint Bixby partnered with James Irvine of San Francisco to buy the almost fifty-thousand-acre Rancho San Joaquin and then parts of two other ranches that together would later become known as the Irvine Ranch. In 1866, on their own, Flint, Bixby & Co. bought the twenty-six-thousand-acre Los Cerritos Ranch for $20,000 in gold and asked Lewellyn's capable younger brother Jotham to

The Bixbys: An Empire of Sheep

manage it, also giving him a future option to buy half the ranch for $10,000.

The sheep prospered on the Cerritos and other ranchos. By 1872, Flint, Bixby & Company was the largest landholder in California, with the exception of the railroad lands. Its interests in eight ranchos totaled 334,000 acres—over five hundred square miles.

In 1869, Jotham exercised his purchase option, and a new company was formed to manage the Cerritos: J. Bixby & Company, half owned by Jotham and half by Flint, Bixby & Co. The new company now had thirty thousand head of sheep, with 200,000 pounds of wool being sent annually to San Francisco via Anaheim Landing, Newport and Wilmington.

Jotham's partners eyed other investments. Lewellyn and Thomas, still living in San Justo, bought the Coast Stagecoach line and invested in a new factory in Alvarado, operated by a fellow Maine emigrant, E.F. Dyer. The factory processed sugar beets into sugar.

Jotham also started buying land on his own. In 1874, he purchased a small interest in Ranchos Palos Verdes, a holding that he later expanded to sixteen thousand acres.

But in 1872, a severe drop in wool prices and another drought in Southern California took a heavy toll on sheep ranchers. Many chose to butcher thousands of newborn lambs rather than lose money raising them. Sheep were sold for twenty-five cents a head, and dressed sheep carcasses could be bought for fifty cents a piece on the streets of many Southern California towns. Flint and Bixby had to borrow funds from their partner, James Irvine. Fortunately, at the Cerritos, Jotham was prepared and was able to withstand the drought by moving all but twelve thousand of the sheep to better grazing lands in San Luis Obispo County.

Flint-Bixby still struggled. In addition to its sheep losses, the company suffered from bad ventures entered into by Benjamin Flint. Thomas and Lewellyn bought him out, and then in 1876, they sold off their share of the San Joaquin to James Irvine for $150,000. A year later, they sold off the Coast Stage Lines.

To hedge his bets, Jotham looked to subdivision of much of his open tracts of land. He donated to and became a board member

A Brief History of Los Alamitos and Rossmoor

The Bixbys kept over twenty-five thousand sheep on the Cerritos rancho, and some Alamitos lands were leased out to smaller sheep ranchers as well. Twice a year, the sheep were driven to the main rancho to be dipped and/or sheared. (Jotham is shown at a sheep dipping in 1872.) In the pen, they would be grabbed, tossed down and sheared of their fleece. The shearer was given a token worth around a nickel, which would later be cashed in. An experienced shearer could shear more than forty animals a day. On the larger ranches like the Cerritos, the shearing season could last a month. *Photography by William Godfrey, courtesy of Rancho Los Cerritos Historical Site.*

of the California Immigrant Union, which promoted settlement and colonization by large groups. Like the Robinson Trust, which had rescued Abel Stearns's fortunes, the Immigrant Union flooded the United States with brochures hyperbolizing the health benefits of California.

The first major real estate venture on Bixby land was undertaken in 1875 with the establishment of the Cerritos Colony, an early subdivision of farm tracts in an area that was generally devoted to stock raising, cattle, sheep, hogs and horses. The choice, rich land—with flowing artesian wells—could be had for $75 to $100 per acre.

The Bixbys: An Empire of Sheep

But while the Immigrant Union had some success at attracting settlers and "colonists"—to Tustin, Pasadena, Orange and Pomona—the biggest boom would come later.

4
THE BIXBYS: TOWN BUILDING

In October 1871, another Bixby from Maine arrived in Southern California. John W. Bixby was not only a first cousin to Lewellyn and Jotham via their fathers but also a first cousin to the Flints through his mother, Deborah Flint.

After graduating from school in Maine in 1868, John W. Bixby worked as a teacher for a short time before heading west. Upon arriving in Los Angeles in early 1871, he found work as a carpenter. When the slowing economy made construction work hard to find, John W. found work at the Cerritos Rancho, beginning like all the Bixbys with the tough job of herding sheep.

In October 1873, John W. Bixby married Susan Patterson Hathaway, the youngest sister of Lewellyn's wife, Mary, and Jotham's wife, Margaret. Susan, who was a few years older than John W., had come to California two years before him. After the marriage, it apparently would not do for the boss's new brother-in-law to be herding sheep, for we hear no more of John W. herding or lambing at the Cerritos.

The newlyweds moved to Wilmington, which by now was incorporated with a population of one thousand and connected by a railroad to Los Angeles. They were almost next-door neighbors of the town's energetic founder, Phineas Banning. John W. continued to work for Jotham, including making improvements for farming, such

The Bixbys: Town Building

as building Clearwater Ditch through Bellflower and present-day Paramount.

John and Susan's first child, Fred Hathaway Bixby, was born in 1875. In that same year, John purchased a portion of the Rancho Canon de Santa Ana in present-day east Yorba Linda.

Living in Wilmington, Bixby met Nathaniel S. Lyon, who along with his brother had obtained a ten-year lease from Michael Reese to herd sheep on part of Rancho Los Alamitos. Lyon would later become California's first forester and gain recognition as a noted botanist and horticulturist. "Hurting badly" from the drought of 1875–76, and with the responsibilities of being newly married, Lyon was motivated to sublease to John Bixby as much Alamitos land as the latter desired.

And John and Susan Bixby desired a lot of it. More railroads were bringing more emigrants to Southern California. John W. knew this meant a larger market, not just for beef and mutton but also for the farm crops and cheese and other dairy products that could be produced on the ranch.

In 1878, he subleased about one thousand acres of Rancho Los Alamitos land from the Lyons. Later that year, Michael Reese, the owner of the Alamitos, died while visiting Germany. His will required that all his property be sold, so when his executors put the Alamitos ranch up for sale, John W. Bixby organized a three-way partnership of himself, J. Bixby and Company (still half owned by Jotham and half by Lewellyn Bixby and Thomas Flint) and banker I.W. Hellman.

Isais W. Hellman was president of the Farmers & Merchants Bank, the largest bank in Los Angeles, and already well on his way to becoming the most important banker on the Pacific Coast. The *Los Angeles Express* reported on December 29, 1886, that Isais paid the most taxes of any man in Los Angeles—more than $14,000.

The new partnership formed the John W. Bixby Company, which in 1881 purchased the 26,392.5-acre Rancho Los Alamitos from the Reese estate for $125,000. The new name also provided further confusion of the Bixby holdings. Since Thomas Flint and Lewellyn Bixby held half interest in the Jotham-managed J. Bixby Company, Flint and Bixby now held half of J. Bixby's one-third interest in the new J.W. Bixby Company.

Bottom line for the Alamitos ranch owners: Lewellyn Bixby and Tom Flint each held a one-twelfth interest, Jotham held a one-sixth interest and Hellman and John W. Bixby each owned a third.

John W. quickly made many improvements to the ranch and its agricultural operations, including a sheep-shearing complex to the southwest of the ranch house. But he focused more and more on other ranch options—building a dairy and cheese-making complex to the northeast, raising horses and swine, and utilizing the railroads to ship breeding stock.

The *LA Times* soon noted the increased productivity of one of the area's most modernized farming operations.

While John W. was having success with his new farming operation on the Alamitos, Jotham's colonizing ventures were facing a rougher path. In 1881, he optioned land to the California Cooperative Colony, which had been trying for six years to start a new town around Clearwater and Hynes (now Paramount). It met with minimal success. And William Wilmore's American Colony and Wilmore City town site along the ocean never took off. However, its potential did attract the attention of Judge Robert Widney, who organized a group of Los Angeles investors—which took over and renamed Wilmore's new town site. They called their company the Long Beach Land and Water Company.

Despite the minimal success of Jotham's ventures, by 1886 Southern California was primed for another real estate boom. Previous booms, descriptive accounts published by the Immigrant Union and the Stearns Ranchos Trust, railway propaganda, newspaper and local agency materials and the work of enthusiastic residents had made the nation aware of Southern California's virtues. The arrival of the Santa Fe Railroad in late 1885 provided the last piece of the puzzle.

Prior to this, the Central Pacific Railroad, and its Southern Pacific subsidiary, controlled virtually all the rail traffic throughout California and much of the traffic through Arizona and on to Texas.

However, by November 1885, the Santa Fe Railroad, utilizing mergers, leases and (by some reports) extortion, completed its cross-country link to Los Angeles. This set off a price war that helped ignite the great boom of the 1880s. At one point, passengers could travel from Kansas City to Los

The Bixbys: Town Building

Angeles for one dollar. That was mainly a publicity stunt that lasted just a day, but travel costs did drop sharply, and soon property values in Los Angeles, Pasadena and the San Gabriel Valley soared.

Santa Monica and other coastal areas were getting attention as well, and John W. was not one to let an opportunity pass by. In 1886, encouraged by his partners, he laid out the five-thousand-acre town of Alamitos Beach, roughly bounded by the ocean on the south, Hathaway Street (now Pacific Coast Highway) on the north, the Los Cerritos boundary line (Alamitos Avenue) on the west and Termino Avenue on the east.

The new town, immediately east of Long Beach, was centered on a two-block-wide strip nearest the ocean. Ocean lots started at $350 and went as high as $600. As distance from the beach increased, so did lot size, up to 160 acres; 60- by 150-square-foot lots were sold in prices ranging from $150 and up, with a $25 down payment.

The timing seemed good. On one January day in 1887, real estate transactions in Los Angeles surpassed $1 million.

But in May 1887, J.W. took ill—presumably appendicitis—and after ten days he died. Susan was devastated and would never wear anything other than widow's black in public ever again.

Within another four months, the real estate boom had died almost as fast as it began. Without the dynamic John W. to operate the Alamitos, the surviving partners decided to separate the ranch into four parts. As the Alamitos Land Company, they would jointly develop the Alamitos Beach town site. As for the rest of the ranch, the J. Bixby Company assumed the northern third adjacent to their Los Cerritos ranch property, roughly north of present-day Stearns and Orangewood Avenues. For all intents and purposes, most of present Los Alamitos was basically part of the Rancho Los Cerritos. I.W. Hellman would get the Orange County land south of the Anaheim Road (current 405 and Garden Grove Boulevard).

J.W. Bixby's heirs kept the middle strip—roughly between the present Pacific Coast Highway and Stearns Avenue in Los Angeles County and between Orangewood and Garden Grove Boulevard in Orange County. This property included the old adobe and the name Rancho Los Alamitos.

A Brief History of Los Alamitos and Rossmoor

Faced with the immediate challenge of raising her young children, Susan Bixby leased the Alamitos ranch lands and stock to Jotham and moved to Northern California, where her son Fred first attended the Belmont Military Academy and later the University of California–Berkeley. Young Fred may have been taken under the wing of I.W Hellman, who by now had also moved to San Francisco to manage the much larger Bank of Nevada (later the Wells Fargo Bank). Hellman's own son, Marco, had graduated from Belmont and was now at UC Berkeley where I.W. Hellman was a member of the Board of Regents. Correspondence shows that Susan trusted Hellman's advice about Fred's education and Alamitos Land Company matters. More than once he reminded her of the importance of her vote at board meetings. Other correspondence shows a rift developing between her and Jotham. A number of family dynamics were at play here. In Susan's mind, Jotham was now getting credit for some of John W.'s progressive ideas. Jotham's son, George H., a recent Yale graduate who was now managing the Alamitos, showed arrogance in some of his actions. And Susan might have had some insecurities and issues in her dealings with her own sisters and the fact that they were married to very wealthy Bixbys.

Susan thought highly of former employee (and another distant Bixby cousin) C.H. Thornburg, who became foreman of the Alamitos Ranch and also the Alamitos Water Company. While Thornburg managed the Alamitos, his sons would frequently follow him all over the ranch land. On Signal Hill, Dwight Thornburg would often find seashells, evidence that the land had once been under water. Twenty-five years later, while working as a geologist for Royal Dutch Shell Company, Dwight remembered the seashells on Signal Hill and recognized that the seismic lift was often an indicator of an underground oil basin.

Although short-lived, the Boom of the 1880s created a population large and independent enough to desire separation from Los Angeles County. In 1889, Orange County was formed over Los Angeles's objections but with the backing of San Francisco, which was eager to detract from the size and prestige of Los Angeles County. Interestingly, Anaheim did not back this separation. It wanted the county line to be farther west at

The Bixbys: Town Building

the Rio Hondo–San Gabriel River so it would be closer to the center of the new county and more likely to be chosen as the county seat. It wasn't, and more centralized Santa Ana became the new county's seat of government.

The new county line roughly followed the shifting sandy beds of Coyote Creek to its confluence with the equally sandy beds of the San Gabriel River. This placed the Alamitos ranch in two counties, a separation that would have significant impacts on the growth and character of the town.

While managing the ranch, George Bixby, still somewhat fresh out of Yale, introduced the Alamitos to "coursing"—weekend parties at the rancho featuring jackrabbit chases where people would come from all over to watch greyhounds chase down hares in life-and-death matches for the rabbits.

In a typical coursing match, a rabbit was released into an open field of about forty acres (slightly smaller than Los Alamitos High School) that was tightly fenced. To give the rabbit "a sporting chance," there was an inner enclosure with twenty to forty "escapes" in which it could flee to safety from the dogs. After the rabbit was given a head start, the dogs were released and then trailed by a man on horseback who assigned points to the dogs' agility catching their prey. If the rabbit wasn't dead when the dogs were through, someone killed it by stepping on its skull.

Newspapers reported that the finely dressed female spectators were more bloodthirsty than the men. Coursing caught on, with the *Times* noting, "The people take to it with a vim that surpassed their enthusiasm for horse racing." The races were then introduced to Los Angeles in the summer of 1897, originally at Agricultural Park, now Exposition Park.

A winning dog might run three races in an hour, get a thirty-minute rest and then race again. *Times* reports mention a dog that was lame and ran on three legs and an eleven-year-old greyhound that won after being dosed with cocaine.

The races in Los Angeles were finally shut down there through the efforts of the Society for the Prevention of Cruelty to Animals and the fact that developers wanted the land to build more housing. But the races at the Alamitos continued infrequently without legal interference until

March 1905, when E.J. "Lucky" Baldwin, whom the *Times* called the "despot of Arcadia," announced plans to stage them on his ranch, now the site of the Santa Anita Racetrack.

Thus ended the Los Alamitos' first foray into organized racing and gambling.

5
THE CLARKS, SUGAR AND A NEW TOWN

According to former Bixby employees, Jotham focused on the Los Cerritos properties (in present north Long Beach and Lakewood), while Lewellyn focused on the eastern Alamitos properties. Lewellyn had a sugar beet connection going back to 1870, when he invested in the first commercially successful sugar beet mill in the United States. This was established in Alvarado, California (about fifteen miles south of Oakland), by E.H. Dyer, another man of Maine.

Although the Alvarado factory successfully produced sugar for some years, it struggled financially. But the Dyers went on to make money by building many sugar beet factories elsewhere.

The process for extracting sugar from certain beets was a relatively young industry. In the later 1800s, to encourage the development of the sugar beet industry, the U.S. government legislated reward bounties. This brought the new industry to the attention of many wealthy men.

Sugar factories were built in the Midwest by the Oxnard brothers, who in 1891 were brought in by Chino Ranch owner Richard Gird to build a factory at that locale. It was the first in Southern California, and farmers as far away as Anaheim, Buena Park and the eastern portions of the Alamitos ranch began growing beets and shipping their raw beets to this factory for processing into refined sugar.

Loading sugar beets into rail cars was a laborious procedure involving a net and a number of hooks, until Anaheim nurseryman Timothy Carroll invented a process involving a hinged wagon and a collapsible side, which reduced dumping time from five minutes to thirty seconds a wagon and labor from three men to two. Carroll's beet dumps were located at the factory and at railroad sites.

At the same time, Los Angeles architect Frank Capitain tried to organize a new sugar factory and cooperative—first, for growers in the Cahuenga Valley near Hollywood and then in the Anaheim area. His work with the Anaheim farmers put him in contact with E.F. Dyer.

The German-born Capitain spent most of his time over the next years pursuing the Anaheim cooperative, filing reports on soil quality and lobbying the U.S. government to renew beet-growing incentives and bounties. Ultimately, neither the Cahuenga nor Anaheim effort took hold.

FRANK J. CAPITAIN.

Frank Capitain was the man most responsible for bringing a sugar beet factory to Los Alamitos. The German-born architect arrived in Los Angeles in 1888, and after designing some improvements to the Chino Sugar Factory, he caught sugar factory fever. After trying to put together cooperatives in Hollywood and then Anaheim, he forged a partnership with the Bixbys and finally, and successfully, the Clarks. Capitain designed the sugar factory, laid out the new town site and oversaw all construction over the first year. His passion must have rubbed some the wrong way. In May 1898, just weeks before the factory's opening, Jotham Bixby replaced Capitain as the Bixby Land Company secretary. He died penniless in a Boulder, Colorado insane asylum in 1901.

The Clarks, Sugar and a New Town

Capitain later told the *LA Times* that the situation needed a single landowner who could force leasing terms requiring the growth of beets. Capitain soon found someone who met these requirements. In October 1893, the *Times* reported that it was "reliably informed" that Claus Spreckels would "erect a sugar house on the Alamitos…he has bonded the tract for six months and paid $1000 on it." For whatever reason, the Spreckels deal went no further, but soon after the *LA Times* reported that Capitain was in contact with Dyer and a "Mr. Bixby." This was most likely Lewellyn.

The Bixbys, working with Capitain and Dyer, pursued financing a sugar beet factory themselves through the Bixby Investment Company and then the Cerritos Land Company. But they were unable to raise the necessary funds as the Bixbys' financial position at the time allowed them to provide land but not capital.

Undaunted, Capitain looked for investors with enough capital to build a sugar beet factory, and early in 1896 he found a party that was not only cash rich but filthy cash rich: William Andrews Clark and J. Ross Clark, bankers of Butte, Montana. William made the family's original fortune, first as a merchant and banker in Montana and then as the owner of copper and silver mines there, as well as in Utah, Nevada and especially Arizona. William A. would later add to his fortune through logging and railroads. In 1901, when he was considered the equal of John D. Rockefeller in terms of wealth, Clark bought himself a U.S. senator's seat (at that time selected by state legislatures) by giving monogrammed envelopes filled with $10,000 to legislators. Hearing that even the U.S. Senate balked at accepting such corruption, Clark "declined" to accept the tainted seat and returned to Montana. He then used a ruse to lure the governor out of state, whereupon the lieutenant governor, a crony, appointed him as senator. Clark's senatorial career was unremarkable except for ultimately leading to reforms on how senators were chosen. Mark Twain considered him vile and corrupt, the "shame of the American nation." Clark himself said he wouldn't trust a man who couldn't be bought. Clark became a widower in the mid 1890s but not a romantic recluse. While in Congress, he married his young "ward," whom he had paid to be educated in France and by whom he had two daughters. After his term, he retired to New York City, built a spectacularly garish home

A Brief History of Los Alamitos and Rossmoor

In the recession of the 1890s, few men had enough capital to build a sugar factory on their own. Two who did were the Clark Brothers of Butte, Montana. Pennsylvania-born William Andrews Clark (left) made his fortune in Montana as a merchant, a banker and then as a copper mine owner. In 1896, he invested in the Los Alamitos Sugar Factory on the advice of his brother J. Ross Clark (right) who moved from Montana to Los Angeles in 1892 for health reasons. Although the deeper-pocketed William was the larger investor and company president, Ross oversaw all the sugar factory operations.

on Fifth Avenue and gaudily spent his increasing fortune, building an art collection that included works by Rembrandt, Rubens, Degas, Titian and Gainsborough. When he died in 1925, although the *New York* Times still called him the fifth-richest man in America, his wealth had won him few friends. His house was torn down, but his art collection was kept intact by the Corcoran Art Gallery in Washington, D.C.

His younger brother J. Ross had his own fortune, some made on his own and some in partnership with William. He moved to Los Angeles in 1892 for his health and invested in a number of enterprises, including oil wells and two banks. In 1896, with the presidential election of the pro-business William McKinley a seeming inevitability, along with a tariff that in effect limited sugar from Cuba, Hawaii and the Philippines, sugar beets looked to be a golden opportunity.

The Clarks were initially given 40 acres (a quarter of a quarter section) for the factory, drainage rights and a promise of 960 more acres once

The Clarks, Sugar and a New Town

WILLIAM A. CLARK	HENRY O. HAVEMYER	WILLIAM K. VANDERBILT	ANDREW CARNEGIE	J. PIERPONT MORGAN	JOHN D. ROCKEFELLER
Copper king.	Sugar king.	Railway king.	Steel king.	Trust king.	Oil king.

MODERN KINGS

As a capitalist, William Andrews Clark ranked high among the "robber baron" hierarchy and was considered the equal of Rockefeller, Carnegie, Morgan and Vanderbilt, as shown by this magazine cartoon from the late 1890s. Mark Twain, who spent much time in Montana, was unimpressed and called Clark "as rotten a human being as can be found anywhere under the flag; he is a shame to the nation." When he died in 1925, he left an estate worth over $600 million.

the factory was built. (The latter land would be the East Ranch, located naturally to the east of the factory where Laurel Park, the Race Track, Cottonwood Church and Costco are now located.)

The Bixbys in turn promised to supply the factory with beets grown on company land, to build a town site and to encourage tenant farmers to buy lots and grow beets to sell to the factory as well. To handle this, the family formed the Bixby Land Company, with Jotham owning 25 percent, Lewellyn and Thomas Flint each holding a 12.5 percent interest and Jotham holding almost 50 percent in trust (the land to be leased or sold). Dyer, Capitain and others also had a small stock ownership.

The Southern Pacific (SP) Railroad was involved from the start, as it would be necessary to get materials and equipment to the new town site, to construct the factory and town and then to transport the sugar after it was processed. The SP drove its usual hard bargains—threatening to bypass Anaheim and run the Alamitos track to Norwalk, unless it got concessions. Capitain and some Anaheim businessmen finally secured the necessary right of ways, and construction on the line was begun and completed in October 1896. The *Times* reported that "Mr. Boshke's crews laid and spiked the rails at an average of 10,000 feet a day, finishing on

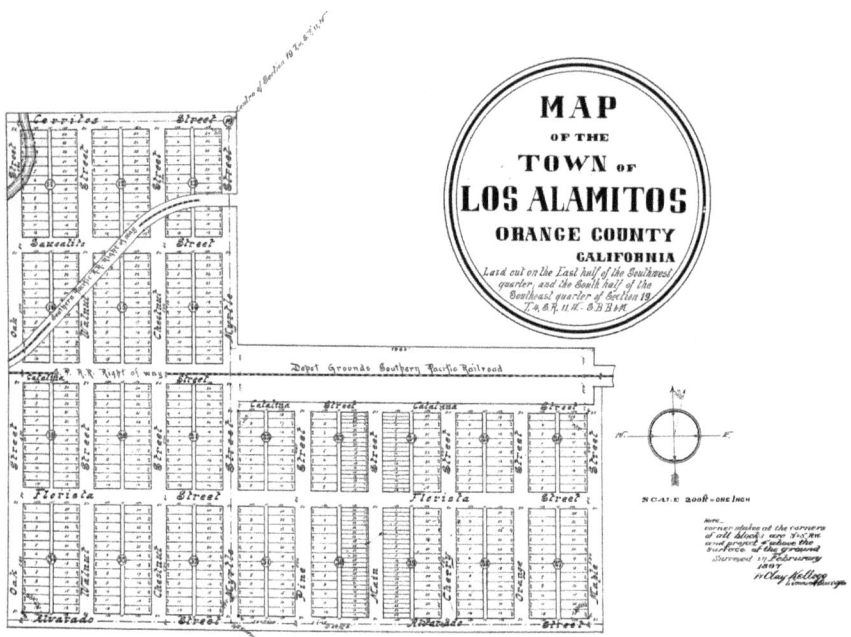

This was Frank Capitain's original layout of the new town. The lots on Main Street (now Reagan) are half width. The rest of the north–south streets are all named for trees (although Myrtle would later become Los Alamitos Boulevard). Note that Katella is called Alvarado, the site of the first successful sugar beet factory in the United States. Lewellyn Bixby had been an investor in that factory, which was built by the Dyers, who were also constructing the Los Alamitos plant. No street extended south of Katella. In mid-1898, I.W. Hellman and Susan Bixby deeded land to the OC supervisors to extend Myrtle south and provide a road from their land and Anaheim Landing to the factory.

October 14, one day ahead of schedule." Telegraph lines went in ten days later. Regular train service over the 9.3-mile spur began on October 28, two trips daily each way to and from Anaheim and connections beyond. In November, it was announced that the grading for continuing the line from Los Alamitos to Long Beach had commenced. Unfortunately, the difficulty of crossing the Coyote Creek and then the New (San Gabriel) River soon caused that effort to be dropped.

But Los Alamitos had already become a bustling town as workers moved in to construct the new town and factory. The *Times* reported that "several enterprising people from Santa Ana have been arranging for lots on which to build a hotel and stores, both dry goods and grocery." Sulfur was discovered in the water of the factory site, and some held out

The Clarks, Sugar and a New Town

The first structure in Los Alamitos was the Southern Pacific Depot. The railroad track from Anaheim was laid and finished in twelve days and immediately after began shipping construction materials, including bricks and machinery necessary to construct the new town and factory. The Depot was located north of Catalina Street, where the present Ganahl Lumber parking lot is located.

hope that the town could also develop as a health resort, if sulfur could be found "at a respectable distance from the smells of the factory." It wasn't.

The *Times* kept a daily watch on the town's progress. On Sunday, November 1 it reported, "About 75 people visited the works at Los Alamitos, and strangers with an 'I'd-like-to-invest sort of air' kept coming and going."

I.M. Marsh was appointed agent for the sale and renting of lots adjacent to the factory; E.H. Dyer and J. Ross Clark were overseeing the placement of the factory's new machinery; the new railroad agent, J.H. Badgely, arrived from Idaho; and the "new restaurant is doing thriving trade catering to 65 permanent borders with the prospect of entertaining a hundred within a week or two. The brain power of the enterprise is F.J. Capitain, who has his offices in the restaurant."

A Brief History of Los Alamitos and Rossmoor

The December 13, 1896 issue of the *Times* noted even more activity:

> *New buildings are going up everywhere…Four weeks ago there was not a new house to be seen on the plain, and now there is a score or more of them. There is also quite a colony of tents. Three-fifths of the people here are from Chino. The one store in the place is conducted by two enterprising men from Tustin, and is a combination barber shop, billiard hall, tobacco stand, stationer's, branch bakery, men's furnishing store, news depot, and laundry office.*

The first completed building in the new town was the $5,000 railroad depot, which was finished in late December. Bridges were built across Coyote Creek to the north on Myrtle (present-day Los Alamitos Boulevard) and Spring Street (Cerritos Avenue) to the west to aid traffic—especially beet deliveries—from the Long Beach and Artesia-Norwalk areas. The town's commissioners predicted there would soon be 150 families located around the new town. Unfortunately, not around to witness this moment was Lewellyn Bixby, who died on December 5 at the age of seventy-one. Jotham Bixby now assumed total control of the Bixbys' Southern California interests.

Dyer carefully oversaw the installation of the new sugar-processing equipment and also visited the Chino factory and rail stops in Anaheim and Buena Park to see how local farmers used the ingenious "beet dump" invention of Anaheim nurseryman Tim Carroll. Dyer ordered one put in place at the Alamitos factory, without compensating Carroll. Machinery, and steel continued to arrive at the factory site, along with bricks—nearly 750,000 of them. In January, the carpenters began to arrive. One was Michael Reagan, whose parents had emigrated from Ireland to New York. Reagan himself had moved in 1889 to Anaheim. Another carpenter was William Butterfield, who moved to the new town with his family of seven. His young children, Harry and Nellie, would write down some of the best descriptions of the young town.

In late January 1897, the first Sunday school service was held, with fifty-two persons present. The *Times* correspondent said, "The sheep ranch of 90 days ago will be the model community and ideal place to live." A month later, the *Times* noted that fifteen thousand pounds of beet seed had been given out to local farmers, and already over one thousand acres had been planted.

Young writer Ralph Bicknell, who visited the town in late spring, left a good description of the young town, describing the new factory as "probably the finest equipped plant in the country." He depicted the town itself as

> *a typical sample of those pyrotechnical Western settlements that yesterday were a wilderness and today are thriving towns—one of those places where everything is put together with shingle nails and mucilage and solidity is as yet unknown. Cheap frame houses were daily being erected; diverse business enterprises were fast making their appearance; cloth tents—temporary dwellings of prospective citizens—were growing up like toad stools in a night.*

The *Times* reported on March 29, 1897, that "already the town feels the need for a schoolhouse which the county supervisors in their wisdom have seen fit to deny." Undaunted, the townsfolk hired teachers to conduct classes in a one-room building that first year. Nellie Butterfield recalled one teacher managing all eight grades: "Several of the older girls helped the younger ones, with their reading or writing. The first teacher was Mr. Keyes, who later finished college, studied law and practiced in Berkeley."

On Sunday, April 25, the *Los Angeles Herald* reported that the town now had a rural hotel kept in very proper order, stores, a post office, a handsome train depot, orderly streets planted with shade trees and a water system with a good head of water. For eight and a half miles, from Signal Hill to beyond Los Alamitos, one could see broad fields ("all of the most vivid green") where the sugar beets were now growing. "Some are now being thinned, others are just being seeded," all on land "which had never felt a plow share until this Spring." Combined with the Anaheim lands, which were growing beets for the Chino factory, the *Herald* said, "for nearly 20 miles east and west and nearly half that north and south, gangs of men and children are seen in knots of fives and tens and twenties,

A Brief History of Los Alamitos and Rossmoor

The Harmona Hotel was the headquarters for Frank Capitain during the town's first days. The hotel was built to last, whereas other entrepreneuring merchants hastily constructed flimsy boardinghouses and tent saloons. At times the Harmona housed the Farmers and Merchants Exchange Club, but it was primarily a hotel and restaurant which remained in business until the 1933 earthquake. Unwilling to spend money on repairs, the owner sold it to the Watts brothers, who moved it to Los Alamitos Boulevard, where they used the bottom floor for their grocery business and the upstairs for their residence and a couple rentals.

weeding or thinning the beets. It is as busy a hive of industry as one has ever seen."

But the young town had its troubles. In late March, Edward Tisnerat, a Los Alamitos boardinghouse and saloon operator of dubious reputation, filed a suit against the Dyers and Clark for $5,000, alleging they had ordered "T. Shadrick, T. Post, Charles Foster, John Hughes and Huffy Duffy and many other employees" to not board at Tisnerat's house or risk being discharged, that Shadrick had already been discharged and that the factory operators had posted notices that Tisnerat "had been driven out of every other place he tried to establish himself in." Perhaps Tisnerat was being referenced when another *Times* report about the same time noted that the Orange city council was very happy to have one of its troublesome bar owners remove to Los Alamitos.

Dyer and J. Ross Clark and Clark spokesman William Holabird maintained that Tisnerat was intimidating other hoteliers. They also indicated that the town's builders preferred that a saloon be part of a large and well-equipped hotel, which would be constructed later that spring. In May Judge Walter Van Dyke ruled against Tisnerat. Other entrepreneurs also saw Los Alamitos's potential for profits via beverages, but Dyer and Clark convinced county officials to reject saloon applications from Anaheim brewer Friedrich Conrad and Alex Gandolfo and John Lagamarsino, who had previously owned a grocery store in Ventura County (although by 1890, Gandolfo was listed on Ventura County records as an "insolvent debtor"). A few months later, the pair ended up buying out Capitan as the owner of the town's first hotel, possibly the Harmona—but Lagamarsino soon shows up back in Ventura County, where he became an early developer. Gandolfo ended up dying in 1918 in Seattle, where he had been in business for a number of years.

The Los Alamitos Sugar Beet Factory, which began processing beets in July 1897, was the first in Orange County. The first campaign was very successful, and the owners expanded the factory, but two years of drought would make the Clarks focus their investments on more predictable financial opportunities. Still the factory was successful enough to encourage others to open four more beet factories in Orange County: Anaheim (1910), Santa Ana (1911) and two in Huntington Beach. By 1915, Orange County was the sugar beet capital of the United States.

A Brief History of Los Alamitos and Rossmoor

One saloon keeper beyond the reach of the town's builders was Peter Tarride, a Frenchman who, with the same Edward Tisnerat, bought five acres west of the factory and the newly straightened Coyote Creek. This property straddled the county line. Tarride started a store on the Orange County side of the line and opened a saloon on the Los Angeles county side, where the factory held less influence. It soon became a hangout for the town's single workers. Tarride started growing some grapes to make wine for his "wine sampling" room, but most of the grapes had to be brought in. To help with this, Tarride hired another Frenchman, Jean Pierre "Pete" Labourdette, who immigrated to the United States in the late 1880s and spent time working the Calico Silver Mine near Barstow before coming to Los Alamitos.

The Los Alamitos factory was considered state of the art. The original plan accommodated three railroad tracks, which led to the main processing area, and the beet sheds. Trams carried raw materials and waste products to and from the main building. Within a few years, electricity was introduced, and much of the machinery and processes were automated. The photo above shows railroad cars delivering the huge quantities of coke and limestone that were used in the kiln processing. This must be from early 1897 because only one smokestack is visible. Five were originally constructed, and when the Clarks doubled the capacity in late 1897, an additional five were added.

The Clarks, Sugar and a New Town

In the second week of July 1897, William A. Clark himself traveled from Montana to visit the town. He visited the factory as part of a grand excursion for members of the Los Angeles Chamber of Commerce. In reporting on the success of the event, and its eminent opening, the *Times* and the *Santa Ana Blade* both noted that the new community now had its own newspaper, the *Los Alamitos Bee*, published by G. Glenn Shaw, formerly of Santa Ana.

It seemed as if all Southern California eagerly awaited the factory's opening, but sadly, one not there to enjoy the moment was Frank Capitan. Just days before the Los Angeles Chamber of Commerce excursion and factory opening, the newspapers reported that George Mohrenstrecher had replaced Capitan as secretary of the Bixby Land Company. It was reported that Capitan had resigned, but it's possible the passionate, independent German's ways did not sit well with the sober

Beets were originally hauled to local sugar factories in six-horse-team wagons, with nets lining the wagon beds. At the station, one side of the net was raised until the beets fell into the waiting rail car. The process involved three to four men and took five minutes per car. In 1894, Timothy Carroll, an Anaheim beet farmer originally from Ireland via Australia, invented a "beet dump" and beet wagon. Teamsters drove a beet wagon onto a raised platform, where it was locked down and then tilted until gravity induced the beets to fall into a waiting rail car. Carroll's invention reduced dumping time from five minutes to only thirty seconds. The Los Alamitos factory used Carroll's system without compensating him, and he sued—and finally won his case in 1907. Carroll also opened one of the first nurseries in Southern California and introduced many Australian trees such as eucalyptus to the region.

style of Jotham Bixby nor with the Clarks, who were used to having their suggestions accepted without question.

On Monday, July 17, 1897, to great fanfare, the factory commenced operations. Beginning at 6:00 a.m. it started processing beets and would operate nonstop twenty-four hours a day (working two shifts) for the next four months, processing twelve tons of beets per hour. Even at this speed, farmers were lined up with their beet wagons along the entire fence behind the factory (on the dirt road called Spring Street), and J. Ross Clark was there to take it all in.

Nellie Butterfield remembered the farmers hauling the beats to the sugar factory, using "a special type of wagon drawn by six horses," and "many of these were seen everywhere while the factory machinery was running and sugar was being made for months in the Fall. Men worked in shifts. Children often went to the factory to take lunch to their father or older brother."

The factory had a successful first year, and enthused by their success, the Clarks immediately contracted with the Dyers to double the processing capability of the factory, from 350 tons a day to 700.

The beet shed was located at the back of the sugar beet factory. Beet farmers lined up their wagons on Spring Street (Cerritos) and entered the shed at the far end. They drove their teams up a ramp to a raised platform, where the wagon was locked down and the platform tilted until gravity induced the beets to fall into a waiting rail car. The entire process took one worker only thirty seconds. The wagon's driver then led his horses out the doors at the front and down the exit ramp.

The Clarks, Sugar and a New Town

To guarantee a consistent supply of beets, they bought from the Bixby Land Company 8,176 acres of Rancho Los Cerritos land just northwest of the factory. It would operate as the Montana Ranch & Land Company. Other syndicates also talked of buying nearby land and opening a second factory. Los Alamitos and its sugar were the talk of Southern California industry, and big things were predicted for the new town.

6
RAILROADS, IMMIGRANTS AND FRED BIXBY

In its 1897 year-end edition, the *Los Angeles Times* labeled Los Alamitos one of the top three towns in Orange County.

Not only was it doubling the capabilities of its factory, but it was also installing a three-thousand-barrel oil tank to provide fuel for the operation of the factory. The doubling of the plant's capacity would require a much larger labor force, and job applicants were arriving and applying daily.

The continuation of the Southern Pacific rail line to Long Beach was considered a sure thing. New merchants, like John Ord, arrived in town to set up shop, a store that Nellie Butterfield remembered as selling "candies and novelties." Job-seekers flocked to the town, and the papers reported a shortage of cottages for factory workers with families. Capitalists and "sugar men" from across the nation and Europe visited the Los Alamitos factory to see the new state-of-the-art factory and bustling new town.

A new two-story schoolhouse was being built, and builder F.L. Spaulding of Los Angeles was pushing to have it finished for the start of school on September 18. The new building had two rooms upstairs and two downstairs. Nellie Butterfield remembered that only the two lower rooms were used, and there were two teachers:

> *Miss Emily Seegmiller for the lower four grades and Miss Ida M. Jones for the upper four grades. Later, Miss Swerdfeger taught the lower*

Railroads, Immigrants and Fred Bixby

This photo is from at least 1915 because it was taken by Edward W. Cochems, a well-known Orange County photographer who moved to the Orange County area in 1915. Santa Ana Main Street (now Reagan Street) in Los Alamitos changed little over the town's first eighteen years. The two main buildings on Main Street were the general store (C.B. Scott Co. Department Store at far right) and the Harmona Hotel (the two-story building just beyond it). Beyond the Harmona was a bakery, the Bixby Land Company office and a drugstore. Across the street on the west (left) side were two billiard parlors (one with a barber chair in front) and a harness shop, a meat market and two tenement hotels.

grades, and Mr. William Henry Cook, whose family lived in Santa Ana, taught the upper grades.

Our brothers went hunting for ducks in Coyote Creek. During the rainy season, they harvested and shipped to Los Angeles mushrooms that grew in the rich soil of the cow pastures near where we lived. They also made collections of bird's eggs found in the willows and trees near Coyote Creek and New River.

The country around Los Alamitos must have been formerly cattle ranches for in the northeast area toward Cypress there were bones of cattle everywhere. School children hunted for them and brought them in as specimens in the study of physiology at school.

During the summer our father took us out where we picked wild berries and grapes in wooded areas northwest of town. We also picked lima beans left for gleaners after the harvest. The family raised

A Brief History of Los Alamitos and Rossmoor

By the early 1920s, the C.B. Scott Company had become the Felts Company. In the 1940s, the building was purchased by Dominie DeBruyn, who operated the Airport Café (now the Boondocks). DeBruyn hauled the building over to the west side of Los Alamitos Boulevard and opened up DeBruyn's Café, which occupied the area where the ReMax Office now sits. In the 1950s, the DeBruyns sold it, and the café was renamed the Los Alamitos Inn.

> *and sold vegetables grown on our two town lots. The boys raised rabbits to sell for meat, and we always kept several cows and sold milk to some of the neighbors.*

Her brother Harry, who would become a noted botanist and professor at UC Berkeley (and later returned to Los Alamitos after he retired), described the downtown:

> *Main Street was a block or so east of the depot and a block south. There was a bakery, a pool room, a vegetable store,* [and] *a grocery store where we could buy nearly everything.*
>
> *...We often went down to Anaheim Landing to fish and have fun on picnics...our boys would take hikes to Coyote Creek where it reached the salt water near the old Fred Bixby place...Coyote Creek was a place*

Railroads, Immigrants and Fred Bixby

Above: Los Alamitos got its first school in 1897, when the Laurel District was formed. For years, this school and its successors were the social center of the community, used not only for school but also for community dances, performances and community meetings.

Right: Laurel School students from the 1907–08 school year.

> *to fish and go swimming. At one point it was dammed up to furnish irrigation water nearby in beet fields.*
>
> *...Our drinking water...around 1897...came from pipes leading from Artesian wells. I recall they drilled a new well not far from where we lived and found artesian water at a depth of 25 feet.*

The *Times* reported that the 1898 Fourth of July was celebrated with a barbecue, baseball game and fireworks display and an evening ball. The description almost seems like a scene out of *Pollyanna* or *The Music Man*. The event had over 700 attendees, and 410 of them took advantage of the sugar factory being open for inspection:

> *All the stores in town were decorated. All the flag poles bore the stars and stripes...*[At the] *factory was an arch over the entrance gate, made of the national colors. The committee provided plenty of ice cold lemonade and the children were supplied with ice cream free in the afternoon...a flagpole 101 feet high was raised, and amid the firing of cannon and the cheers of the people the Stars and Stripes were unfurled.*

The day's events began with a program in the church at 10:00 a.m., which included a prayer, a reading of the Declaration of Independence and a number of songs performed by locals—including two versions of "The Star-Spangled Banner" and concluding with the audience joining in for a version of "America." They moved outside for a bicycle race, a potato sack race, an egg race, a fat man's race and a one-hundred-yard race for boys and the five-inning baseball game between the "lean team and the fat team," with the latter winning by three runs. The day concluded with fireworks at 7:30 p.m. and a "grand ball" in the hall of the Bixby-owned Los Alamitos Improvement Company, "at which about sixty couples were present." The music was supplied by Messrs. Bunyard and Freeman.

The presence of Oscar Bunyard alone guaranteed a good turnout. Bunyard was a fiddle player from Cypress, and it was said by many old-timers that it wasn't a good party unless Oscar was playing the fiddle.

But rough times soon came to Los Alamitos.

Railroads, Immigrants and Fred Bixby

The first religious services in Los Alamitos were held outdoors and in tents, but in early 1898, the Bixby Land Company donated land for a Union Church (a building used by multiple denominations). The building eventually came to be called the Community Church.

The oldest known still-standing house in Los Alamitos is located on Chestnut Street and is believed to have been constructed in 1897. It is now known as the Layton House, since former blacksmith Leo Layton and his wife, Florence, lived in it for many years after buying it in the 1940s. Layton also served as the chief of the Los Alamitos Volunteer Fire Department for over thirty years, and Florence headed up that unit's ladies' auxiliary for many years as well.

Unfortunately, the second year's crop suffered from a lack of rain, and the sugar factory was only open for ten days.

Life was not easy on the desolate farmland and worse during a drought. Coyotes howled constantly, and brazen ones jumped on barrels to look in cabin windows. The monotonous wind and loneliness led to more than one farm wife attempting suicide. Mrs. Elisha Gooden went insane after her oldest son was killed on the train tracks. In December, the first of a few charity balls was held in Los Alamitos to help those whose crops failed in the drought.

Sudden death was not uncommon in the Mexican community. In late July, factory employee Santiago Martinez killed his younger first cousin, Locario Martinez, who after being caught having a relationship with Santiago's wife tried to sneak back and kill the older cousin.

In 1897, The Bixby Land Company's advertising had lured a number of German Russians (Germans who had migrated to Russia during the reign of Catherine the Great) to grow beets east of Los Alamitos. The 1898 drought was bad enough, but a second year made things so bad that in late April 1899, some German-Russians snuck away in the middle of the night, leaving behind over $15,000 in debt and causing animosity among Anaheim merchants and the remaining German Russians, most of whom eventually left the area as well.

The Clarks were sued by Anaheim inventor Timothy Carroll, who claimed that factory general manager E.F. Dyer had used his beet dump invention at the Los Alamitos plant and on surrounding rail lines without paying Carroll any royalties. It would take almost ten years, but in 1907 Carroll won his lawsuit.

And south of town, the other Alamitos partners were not happy. The John W. Bixby heirs would claim they did not learn of the original factory contract—nor the granting of a right of way across their property—until it was printed in the San Francisco papers. (This seems a stretch. Even though Susan and her children were living in northern California while young Fred attended UC Berkeley, and Jotham Bixby had been leasing their Alamitos lands for $6,000 per year, there were still newspaper stories in the San Francisco papers, correspondence with Hellman and rumors aplenty before the deal was announced.) After the successful first campaign, in October 1897, Hellman wrote to Jotham and George Bixby on behalf of some Hellman tenants about getting factory beet contracts for five hundred acres. George wrote back on behalf of his father saying that regrettably it couldn't be done. With the Clarks' purchase of over eight thousand acres, they could now almost supply all their own sugar beets for the factory. Not all the land was planted in beets; much was planted in alfalfa and vegetables or used as pasture for the dairy cattle, sheep and pigs. Nonetheless, the Los Cerritos Bixbys (i.e., Jotham, and the heirs of Lewellyn) had to reduce their own beet contracts by one thousand acres.

Tenants on Susan Bixby's land also could not obtain beet contracts, so Susan and Hellman entertained efforts to seek the construction of a second factory in the area. In October, Hellman was asked by an Anaheim businessman to commit enough acreage to sugar beets to induce the Oxnards (who had already expressed interest) to build a new factory near Hellman's lands. Hellman liked the project but couldn't commit because his land was all leased out. Any commitment would have to come from the tenant farmers.

But in February 1898, Hellman signed an option with *Los Angeles Times* publisher Harrison Gray Otis (who had partnered with a Dutch sugar beet syndicate) for the sale of all of Hellman's Alamitos lands for $650,000. About the same time, Susan Bixby optioned her property to William Holabird, who often worked with the Clarks but this time seemed to be working with an English syndicate. In addition, J. Ross Clark talked openly about building a second factory nearby. But then the Dutch were scared off by the outbreak of the Spanish-American War, and after the bad 1898 season, the Clarks (and Holabird) decided against building a second factory. So the J.W. Bixby heirs and Hellman were out the sale of any of their land and still had no beet contracts.

To add insult and odor to injury was the apparent smell of the creek water—laden with factory waste—that passed by Susan Bixby's adobe home. The level terrain minimized any current that might swiftly carry inky factory waste to the ocean. Unable to stand the smell—at least while they had no contract for beets—Susan (and her willing or unwilling children, Fred and Susanna) sued to deny the Clarks the use of Coyote Creek and the San Gabriel River on their property. The Clarks filed a suit of their own—against Jotham Bixby for failing to secure a right of way from Susan, as promised in their original contract with the Bixby Land Company. It went to trial in 1901. The jury heard plenty of testimony, including some from local farmers, that the smell was not much different from the other farm smells in the area. Ultimately, the jury returned no verdict.

The Clarks also became fully aware of the strength of the Sugar Trust, led by Henry Havemeyer on the East Coast and the Spreckels interests on the West Coast. As J. Ross Clark, no stranger to hardball business tactics, matter-of-factly later explained to Congress, "The big companies set the price, if we fight them they'll undercut us till we go out of business." So the Clarks settled into a truce that avoided price competition and guaranteed a profit for Clark's Sugar but left little room to expand its market.

The Clarks shifted their attentions to more lucrative areas—real estate and railroads. Both were very present around Los Alamitos and Long Beach thanks to Henry Huntington's—and Isais Hellman's—development of the Pacific Electric Railroad.

In 1898, after the death of his uncle Collis Huntington, Henry lost a boardroom battle for control of the Southern Pacific Railroad to E.H. Harriman, owner of the Union Pacific. Undaunted, Henry set his sights on Southern California, funded and advised by Hellman, the Rancho Los Alamitos co-owner and now also the president of the Wells Fargo Bank. The "Huntington-Hellman syndicate," as newspapers of the time called them, already owned electric street railroads in San Francisco and Los Angeles. In May 1901, Hellman wrote to Huntington, "I think the time is on hand when we should commence building suburban railroads out of the city [Los Angeles]," adding that he [Hellman] had already commenced a survey of potential routes. Electric railroads provided opportunities not only in transportation but also in electrical power and real estate.

The initial plan included consolidating their small electric railways in south Los Angeles and then extending them—first to Long Beach and then down the coast to Newport Beach. It was undoubtedly no coincidence that this would make Hellman's Alamitos lands along the ocean far more valuable.

Railroads, Immigrants and Fred Bixby

I.W. Hellman, the most influential Pacific Coast banker from the 1870s to 1920, played a major role in the development of the Los Alamitos area. He invested in John W. Bixby to purchase the Rancho Los Alamitos. He partnered with Henry Huntington to bring the Pacific Electric Railroad to Southern California in general and Long Beach and Seal Beach in particular. He helped relocate the amusement area of the 1915 San Francisco Panama-Pacific Exposition to the Seal Beach Joy Zone.

Well aware of the Pacific Electric's (PE) proposed route, Hellman's long-time land agent, Philip A. Stanton, organized a group to buy property south of the Bolsa Chica mesa, subdivide it and sell lots as the new town of Pacific City. These plans were delayed when the PE was spectacularly outbid for an existing rail franchise in south Los Angeles. Its competition turned out to be the Clarks, later revealed as acting as a front for Harriman. The ridiculous price sent a strong message that Harriman would not let Huntington-Hellman undercut the Southern Pacific.

Another challenge was the Bolsa Chica Gun Club. In 1898, some Los Angeles businessmen bought oceanfront land on the mesa south of Hellman's Ranch for a hunting club. They opposed a railroad through the site—at least at the price they were offered. Undaunted, Huntington said he would run his line to Newport Beach inland to Santa Ana and then south.

Stanton, now a Republican assemblyman from Los Angeles, saw his ambitions threatened and arranged a compromise: Huntington and some PE partners got memberships in the exclusive Bolsa Chica club whose members received an improved offer—and other perks—for granting rail rights to the PE. To further lure Huntington to continue his line down the coast, the Pacific City partners agreed to buy out Stanton, give that stock to Huntington and rename their city Huntington Beach. Stanton took his money and partnered with wealthy I.A. Lothian to buy the land just north of Anaheim Landing from Hellman and Susan and Fred Bixby. Stanton, Lothian and some minor partners (including key Pacific Electric executives including Huntington) formed the Bayside Land Company and the new town of Bay City (later Seal Beach).

The Pacific Electric reached Long Beach in July 1902. Huntington, by all accounts a very knowledgeable railroad man, called it "the finest railroad in the world." Initially, it would be the Pacific Electric's most profitable line (although most of that was from freight). Long Beach was soon followed by Bay City (Seal Beach) in 1904 and Huntington Beach and Newport Beach in 1905. This set off a real estate boom along the Long Beach and Orange County coast. One of those encouraged by Bay City's prospects was Los Alamitos storekeeper John Ord, who in February 1904 hauled his two-story building down the road from Los Alamitos to become Bay City's first resident.

But Huntington's insistence on not declaring profits to investors (instead opting to reinvest PE profits into further expansion) caused the Hellman syndicate to sell its controlling share to Harriman, making the PE and SP basically one railroad after 1905. Harriman allowed Huntington almost free reign with his newer, faster electric PE as long as it didn't threaten the slower, coal-powered SP. But Huntington still owned the lucrative electric power companies that provided power to the new communities, as well as the rail lines, and the local real estate he was given in return for bringing an electric railroad to a community. For Huntington, the PE was a device to increase the value of his electric and real estate operations. Nonetheless, he totally sold out to Harriman in 1910.

The "Red Cars" reduced travel time to downtown Los Angeles and brought day-trip visitors and buyers to the new beach towns—Naples, Alamitos Bay, Bay City, Sunset Beach and Huntington Beach—in which Huntington, not so surprisingly, had a financial stake. Still, as a passenger line, despite the romanticism of later advocates, the PE never turned a profit. It was only profitable via freight.

The PE also built an inland branch line running from Watts Station to Santa Ana. Where the line crossed Walker Street, the core of the new community of Cypress was born. Benedict Station, where it crossed the Anaheim–Los Alamitos line and later junctioned with the spur line to Smeltzer/Huntington Beach, became the center of Stanton. (For Los Alamitos residents, this also became the quickest rail connection to downtown Los Angeles. Take the SP to Benedict and catch the PE to downtown Los Angeles.) But the growth of all these communities—inland, and especially along the coast—was severely retarded by the 1906 San Francisco earthquake and fire. Most available investment dollars were diverted north, where bigger profits could be made as that city rebuilt itself.

But the PE kept expanding. The enlarged network of railroads also provided a solution to the acute California agricultural labor shortage. Railroad-connected labor contractors began shipping in Mexican workers through El Paso. From there, they rode the Southern Pacific to Arizona or Southern California, where they were shipped to local farms on Pacific Electric lines.

The chaos of the Mexican Revolution of 1910—especially in the Jalisco-Guadalajara area—forced many Mexican peasants north to the United States to find work. The 1900 census shows few Mexican workers residing full time in Los Alamitos, although some were definitely here, as Congregational Church circuit minister Alden B. Case noted of his visits to Los Alamitos:

> *The majority of the laborers are Mexicans. Only a few of these are residents of the village. They come from near and far. One company of twenty men come all the way from Michoacan, which is one of the most distant states of Mexico. They tell me they expect to return home in December.*
>
> *Some of these people find cheap houses to rent in the village, but most of them live in tents or booths. Groups of these called "campos" are found here and there, each containing twenty, thirty or more laborers, some accompanied by their families. These camps are located wherever convenient for work, usually near water and under spreading trees.*

Case held services in the field, often using a "stereopticon" (an early slide projector) to attract crowds. "An ordinary religious meeting would attract few of them, but the lantern views of Mexico draw everybody."

The minister noted that "the Mexicans gathered here are of the roughest class. One outdoor meeting was interrupted by a scuffle, in which pistols were drawn." This was not an isolated incident. An April 1903

A Brief History of Los Alamitos and Rossmoor

LA Times article noted, "Los Alamitos contains a colony of about 75 to 100 Mexicans. In the past five years there have been more than a dozen murders and murderous assaults among them." Most attacks took place in the camps, but on occasion violent crime found its way into the city streets.

From late August to early October 1907 the *LA Times*, with its penchant for exaggeration, ran such headlines as: "Los Alamitos at War" and "Bad Cholo Gun Men Unchecked, Riotous." In August, respected deputy constable Juan Orosco had been shot by a transient worker at a Saturday night dance. (Incidentally, this would make Orosco the first authorized and paid peace officer to be killed in the line of duty in Orange County, preceding the generally credited Robert Squires by five years.) The paper also noted that the "good Mexican population" was appalled at the murder of their "protector." A few weeks later, after the killer got off on manslaughter charges, the *Times* again reported that the "carousing, gun-loving Mexican population" celebrated with a night-long "carnival of wine and shooting in the Mexican quarter of the sugar factory hamlet." Authorities in Orange County and Long Beach blamed much of the problem on the winery now owned by Pete Labourdette.

Things calmed down after this as the local Mexican population stepped up to police the area themselves and a new half-Mexican constable, C.W. Moore, brought order to the area. The transient workers usually lived in a tent city located just southeast of the factory (where Trend Printing and part of the hospital are now located), but more and more Mexican families established permanent residence in homes on Pine or farther west on Walnut (at that time the western edge of town). Many descendants of these first families are still in town: the Torres, Lujans, Napoles, Sisneros, Zamarippas and Guzmans, to name a few.

As the Mexican families settled and stayed, Los Alamitos came to have a relatively low number of transient field workers compared to other farming communities. Congressional testimony in 1920 showed that where the Oxnard, Chino and Anaheim sugar plants needed around 1,000 migrant workers annually; Huntington Beach, 1,300; and Santa Ana, 600, the fields around Los Alamitos needed only 400.

Peter Tarride's saloon, now owned by Jean Pierre Labourdette (called Pete by most), continued to draw the attention of local police.

Railroads, Immigrants and Fred Bixby

This page: The family with the oldest roots in Los Alamitos are the Labourdettes. Jean Pierre Labourdette (top), a native of Bellocq, in Southern France, came to Los Alamitos in 1898 after stops in New Orleans and the Calico mine near Barstow. He took a job at Peter Tarride's winery and saloon. On a trip to a Chino vintner to buy grapes, Labourdette met a housemaid who also hailed from Bellocq. Within a few months, Eunice Domercq and Pete were married, and she joined him in Los Alamitos. In 1900 they bought out Tarride. Pete and Eunice raised a large family, whose descendants now include not only the Labourdettes but also Poes, Sjostroms, Bergs and many others.

A Brief History of Los Alamitos and Rossmoor

Labourdette was born in Bellocq, France (just north of the Pyrenees and Basque provinces), in 1864 and immigrated to the United States around 1890. After stops in New Orleans, and working the Calico mine near Barstow, he took a job at Tarride's new Los Alamitos saloon and winery. His duties included delivering and picking up materials from inland towns. While visiting a Chino vintner to buy grapes, Labourdette met a housemaid who also hailed from Bellocq. Within a few months, Eunice Domercq and Pete were married, and she joined him in Los Alamitos. In 1900, he and Eunice bought out Jean Tarride before the latter returned to France.

Even under the new ownership, the "winery" often ran afoul of authorities. After a 1905 incident, one local city attorney said, "It's no winery. There's not a grape or vine within three miles of the place. It's a blind pig pure and simple." (A blind pig was slang for an establishment where one paid to see an entertainment—such as a blind pig—and alcoholic beverages were given as a "courtesy" to customers. Since alcohol was not sold, the establishments theoretically were not subject to the same scrutiny as saloons.) Whether Labourdette ever featured blind pigs is not known, but his grandson, Leon Sjostrom, says Pete would frequently host boxing matches at his saloon. Pete and Eunice would raise seven children in Los Alamitos, and three of them still have descendants there: Labourdettes, Sjostroms and Poes.

Sugar was not the only product of the factory. The Bixbys and Clarks realized the potential of sugar beet pulp as feed for cattle. In December 1899, the *Times* reported that 150 sheds were constructed in Los Alamitos for dairy cows "to be fed on sugar factory leavings."

In 1903, Jotham Bixby built a dairy (where Los Alamitos High School is now located) and hired Louis Denni, a Swiss immigrant and trusted employee, to run it. The dairy's shed accommodated over 200 cows, and more were corralled in the area between the factory and Coyote Creek. In July, the first of 1,200 cattle were brought via railroad from Arizona to fatten on the factory pulp and molasses and replenish the fields with manure. In August, local newspapers told of a big cattle drive in 1903 from the Chino Hills area through Brea Canyon. The cowboys spent the night near Buena Park before continuing on to Los Alamitos the next day,

Railroads, Immigrants and Fred Bixby

In 1896, one of the first town lots to be purchased was by a Frenchman, Peter Tarride, and Edward Tisnerat, a man of questionable reputation. The lot was located a quarter mile west of the factory site and conveniently straddled the county line. The pair established a winery on the Orange County side and opened a saloon on the Los Angeles County side, thus beyond the reach of the more conservative Orange County lawmakers. The Tarride saloon did good business among the rough beet field workers and was the site of many knife fights, some of which resulted in deaths. In 1900, Tarride sold the winery and saloon to Pete and Eunice Labourdette, but even with the change of ownership, the saloon did not enjoy a good reputation among local authorities.

where they herded the cattle into large pens constructed for the purpose. In December 1903, over 800 cattle were in Alamitos to fatten at the factory feed lots before being sent to slaughterhouses.

South of Los Alamitos, the J.W. Bixby Ranch took on new life under the energy of Fred Bixby. He graduated from the University of California in 1898, married his classmate Florence Green and assumed management of his family's Alamitos lands and its positions on the boards of most Bixby-related companies. Fred also revealed plans to continue his father's ambition of making the Alamitos a "working cattle ranch" and not subdividing the land (in contrast to only a year before, when Susan entertained offers of selling their entire acreage to Holabird's English syndicate and then the Clarks).

Although unsure of himself at first, and perhaps intimidated by the ambitions of his mother, Fred grew into the job. He and J. Ross Clark resolved their legal issues with the factory dumping much of its waste on their East Ranch lands, where the Cottonwood Church and the racetrack are now located, and also contracting to buy beets from Bixby and Hellman tenants. Hellman soon entrusted the management of his Alamitos property, and then other ranches, including the large Nacimiento Ranch in Central California, to Fred. By the 1920s, Fred was one of the leading ranchers in America and was an adviser to President Calvin Coolidge.

More and more of Fred's early tenants were Belgian farmers. While the number was significant, the size of this group is often overstated; 1920 Los Alamitos census reports show only twenty-one heads of households of Belgian birth. The only Belgian-born resident in the 1900 Los Alamitos area census was Charles Vlasschaert, a farmer who emigrated in 1895, soon joined by his brother Petrus. Richard Longeval arrived in 1901 to work at the factory, and that same year the *Los Angeles Times* reported

After graduating from UC Berkeley "by a narrow squeak" in 1898, Fred Bixby returned south to become one of Southern California's most prominent citizens. He continued his father's dream of making the Alamitos a modern, profitable working ranch and earned the respect of I.W. Hellman, the Clarks and the tenant farmers on his lands. Fred became influential in area politics and was an adviser to U.S. president Calvin Coolidge on national agricultural issues. He and his wife, Florence, lived in the Rancho Los Alamitos adobe for almost fifty years, overseeing the operations of his Fred Bixby Ranch Company. After his death in 1952, the company, now renamed the Bixby Ranch Company, still remained a major player in Long Beach, Rossmoor and Seal Beach issues.

Railroads, Immigrants and Fred Bixby

that an unidentified "Belgian laborer" had assaulted a customer at Pete Labourdette's saloon.

Vlasschaert wrote back to Belgium about the Los Alamitos area, and neighbors and relatives from his hometown began showing up—especially after 1906. They included Emile Baeskens (who worked for the Vlasschaerts); Rene Baeyens; Gustave Beerens (and his wife, Caroline Goessens); Rene Cannau; Camile Cauwel; Ivo Cosyns, his father-in-law Lawrence Lerno and his friends, the three Vandemaele brothers; and Oscar Watte. Other Belgians, inspired by letters from the likes of Camil Wuytens ("Come to California. This is the earthly paradise."), soon followed. These included the DeBruyns, DeCraemers, DeVuyst and Ottes (1909). Once here, most of the Belgians stayed with farming and leased land off Bixby Road (present-day Main Way, running due East to Stanton and Garden Grove) or to the south and grew beets, barley and lima beans. Many would have to move when the military bases were built in the early 1940s.

Although a few individual Flemish-Americans were here before, most of the twenty or so Belgian families who settled around Los Alamitos arrived after 1905 and farmed the area a few miles south of Los Alamitos. Oscar Watte and his wife, Anna, leased this farmhouse from the Fred Bixby Ranch Company. It was located on Bixby Road (now Main Way), a little to the west of the present Sprouts store. The Wattes lived in the farmhouse until 1959, when they moved out, and it was removed to make way for a later phase of Rossmoor.

A Brief History of Los Alamitos and Rossmoor

The children of the Mexican and Belgian families attended Laurel School, where English was the only language allowed to be spoken in class. Those caught speaking anything else would be dismissed or made to stand in the corner. All the children were friendly to one another, but some old-timer accounts indicate that the immigrant children tended to stick together, so it was up to the native-born whites to "make friendly" or initiate any conversations among them.

After two tough years of drought, the Los Alamitos Sugar Company prospered. E.F. Dyer moved on to focus on building new beet sugar mills, and he was replaced as superintendent by H.C. Lawrence, who oversaw the introduction of many innovations, especially in automation, and all well chronicled in the sugar industry journals. Chief engineer F.K. Edwards devised a system to generate electricity from the waste steam in the evaporation process—enough to power all the pumps inside the factory and six of the eight exterior artesian wells. Electric cars were brought in to carry pulp to the silo, electric sewing machines stitched shut the sacks of sugar, electric-powered automatic shutdowns were installed and electric stackers were constructed in the warehouses.

In the Administrative Building, systems were put in place by office manager A.W. Jones so that two men could handle the work that once took five.

In the field, longtime agricultural chief James L. Elam perfected crop-rotation systems to minimize the damage of the nematode worm and curly top virus. Factory waste, sometimes combined with refuse lime, was piped out a couple miles to the beet fields to provide irrigation and fertilizer.

The impact of droughts was lessened by the increasing number of artesian wells, over thirty in the area and five on the Los Alamitos factory grounds alone. Many of these were now drilled by Michael Reagan. The former factory carpenter had begun buying out the Bixby Land Company's water system, and by 1910 he was running the local water company.

With the factory operations in good hands, the Clarks focused their attention on their other operations. As noted earlier, William A. was finally selected as a senator from Montana—albeit not an ideal one—and after his one term he moved to New York, where he built a spectacularly garish mansion near Central Park. He did not let his political obligations interfere with his business. His United Verde Mine in Arizona reportedly was still earning a profit of $400,000 a month ($10 million in present dollars). William and J. Ross also undertook the construction of a Salt Lake to Los Angeles Railroad—and building the city of Las Vegas in the process. (It would later be learned that around 1904 they sold out a majority interest to E.H. Harriman's Union Pacific monopoly while they continued for about eight years to act as a front.) By 1910, Clark would begin selling out his Montana mines to the Anaconda Company.

As for the Alamitos, around 1908 J. Ross started grooming his son Walter Miller Clark in the factory operation, making him an assistant manager in 1909. In 1912, J. Ross even bought a home across from the sugar factory and was remodeling it to house young Clark and his bride and newborn son. He barely had a chance to reside in it. He died as one of the passengers who went down with the *Titanic* on April 14, 1912.

7
OIL, SUGAR BLUES, HORSE MEAT AND EARTHQUAKES

From 1911 through 1920, Orange County was the sugar bowl of the United States. The county had more factories and more beet acreage and produced more sugar than any other county in the nation. It brought in five times the revenue of the county's most famous product—oranges—and was the main crop in the area currently roughly bordered by the county's main freeways: the Long Beach (710), San Diego (405) and Santa Ana (I-5) freeways.

As noted earlier, Los Alamitos was an industry leader in quality and innovation. Alone, it produced enough sugar to supply the Los Angeles market. Its success was enough to inspire the construction of four more factories in Orange County: the Santa Ana Cooperative in 1908 and three in 1910 (Anaheim, May; Huntington Beach; and the James Irvine–controlled Santa Ana Sugar Company, December).

In 1914, the experienced Ernest C. Hamilton was hired to manage the Los Alamitos sugar factory. Over the next ten years, he continued to upgrade factory equipment and had more cottages built to house factory workers with families. For the unmarried workers, a two-story structure was built that included many recreation facilities downstairs. In addition to tennis courts, he ordered the clearing of small farm lots for children. Hamilton and some wealthy Long Beach friends (including some of the Hatch family who ran the First Security Bank) established the Farmers

Oil, Sugar Blues, Horse Meat and Earthquakes

In 1914, Ernest C. Hamilton was hired to manage the Los Alamitos Sugar Factory. Hamilton upgraded much of the equipment and instituted many changes to the factory grounds, including adding cottages for workers with families and a clubhouse to house single workers. He also built a playground for factory and town children, a tennis court and croquet grounds. Above, a woman and her two children stand in front of their cottage home on Serpentine Drive.

Gun Club, a duck-hunting club located about a mile northeast of the factory. In addition to Hamilton, other Los Alamitos members included assistant factory superintendent Gus J. Strodthoff and Dick Ables.

Strodthoff had been working for the factory since day one, beginning as a young office clerk, and had worked his way up to the number two spot. He came from Anaheim, where his father, a German immigrant, managed the water company. Strodthoff also spent a few years in Arizona working for the Clarks' United Verde mining operation in successive positions of increased responsibility.

The plant superintendent was Karl V. Bennis, a Maine native who started at the factory in 1903, after learning the craft of "sugar boiling" at a beet factory in Ogden, Utah. Bennis proved his worth through a couple inventions, winning a lawsuit over a shock absorber, and in 1910 he took the first-ever auto trip through the Anza Borrego Desert, a region he returned to many times. In 1921, when a major fire broke out at the sugar factory warehouse, Bennis's quick response minimized the damage.

Unfortunately, while rescuing a worker from a room filled with caustic gas, he damaged his lungs. The dry desert heat became more attractive, and he eventually became one of the poets and unofficial publicists of Anza-Borrego Desert Park.

The 1921 fire consumed over half of Los Alamitos's sugar production that year, but Hamilton had the warehouse's rear wall rebuilt, stronger than ever—in concrete. The wall is still visible from Los Alamitos High School on Cerritos Avenue (behind Volcano Burgers). It now houses the Grating Pacific Company.

Another employee assuming more responsibility was Ohio-born William Poe. He began with the company around 1905 as a chemist, and by 1918 he was the chief engineer. He was the first of four Poes by that name to play an influential role in Los Alamitos business, government and social affairs.

Another E.C. Hamilton innovation was to host pancake breakfasts and barbecues to celebrate the start and finish of each season's sugar beet–processing campaign. After the "banner" 1916 campaign, one trade publication noted: "The annual barbecue for the beet growers and factory men, and their families, will be held at the famous Montana Ranch… located seven miles from the factory." Events included "a baseball game, running races, sack races, three-legged races, tug of war, and last but not least, the "greased Pig." The ballgame was "between the farmer boys and a picked team from the factory…[undoubtedly seeking] revenge for the terrible drubbing given them by the farmers last year."

Oil, Sugar Blues, Horse Meat and Earthquakes

Bruno Juskjievicz, an immigrant from Poland (via stops at sugar factories in Michigan and Idaho), came to Los Alamitos to take over as agricultural superintendent. Juskjievicz was an expert on breeding beet seeds. After the world war interrupted the importation of beet seeds, J. Ross Clark brought him to California to breed beet seeds that were sold to beet factories around the country.

Bruno's wife, Bessie, who would become very active in the town, remembered all the six-horse wagons carrying beets to the factory, most wearing bells. "You could hear them a long way away."

Because of the shortage of homes in the community, Bruno and Bessie spent their first years living in the clubhouse. They got to know J. Ross Clark and his wife, who told them they spent over $1 million to find the body of their son after he went down with the *Titanic*. Prior to Walter's fateful trip, J. Ross Clark had bought a home at Chestnut and Catalina

William Poe, who came from Ohio to Los Alamitos in the early 1900s, was one of the area's earliest drivers. At this time, all the town's roads were dirt. But by 1918, four miles of Los Alamitos Boulevard had been paved, and it had become a main route from the San Gabriel Valley to the beach communities, designated as State Highway 35. This picture was taken circa 1920. William Poe Jr. is seated on his father's lap. Four generations of Poes have lived in Los Alamitos and been influential in city affairs.

from the widow of the former Sugar Factory auditor, A.W. Jones. It was the only factory-owned home west of the boulevard. J. Ross was fixing it up for Walter, who was assuming more responsibility with the factory, and his young bride and newborn child. After Walter disappeared on the *Titanic*, the Clarks maintained the house for a few years; then they offered it to the Juskjieviczs, who bought it and lived there for over sixty years.

Hamilton also improved the company's electrical-generating capability. The power plant was located across Los Alamitos Boulevard. It not only supplied power to the factory but also provided Southern California Edison with surplus power.

Clark's Extra Fine Sugar sold well in two-pound, five-pound and one-hundred-pound sacks. The Sugar Company, the local farmers and the town's businesses all thrived. Some, like Karl Bennis, teacher Ada Espe and factory worker Heliodor Torres, bought cars and traveled the area's few

Sacking the refined sugar. Seventeen hours from the time the raw beet enters the factory through the flume, it drops from the granulator (right) into the sacks, as shown in this picture. Every sack shown here contained one hundred pounds of sugar, but it was also available in two-pound sacks. From this station, the sacks were trucked to the great warehouse adjacent to the factory. One report said the Los Alamitos factory produced enough sugar to supply the entire Los Angeles area, but much of the product ended up being sold in the Midwest.

Oil, Sugar Blues, Horse Meat and Earthquakes

paved roads. Because it went from Norwalk to Seal Beach, Los Alamitos Boulevard became the town's main street, and local businessmen, like James and George Watts, who had taken over the Felts' general store, moved their businesses there from Main Street. Los Alamitos Boulevard was soon paved, and as State Route 35, it became a main auto route for people traveling from Pasadena and the San Gabriel Valley to the beach. In 1931, blacksmith Richard Longeval, whose shop was at the corner of Los Alamitos Boulevard and Spring Street, took advantage of his heavily traveled location by converting his site to a gas station.

In the winters, floods still inundated the area every few years, prompting prepared families like the Labourdettes to bring out the rowboat they kept for such emergencies.

Anaheim Landing was originally established as a port by Anaheim winemakers to ship their wine and import lumber and other products. But as shipping soon went through the port of Wilmington and newly arrived railroads, Anaheim Landing became a resort and picnic spot for the locals, including those from Los Alamitos. With the founding of Bay City (Seal Beach) in 1903 and the construction of the Joy Zone (the roller coaster and amusement park, which was imported from the 1915 Panama-Pacific Exposition in San Francisco), all of Seal Beach became a popular getaway for Los Alamitos residents. As late as 1924, the *Press-Telegram* reported that "half the town of Los Alamitos picnicked for a day at Seal Beach."

A Brief History of Los Alamitos and Rossmoor

During the summer, those with cars sometimes took Sunday drives to Anaheim Landing, or beginning in 1916 they went to Phil Stanton's new amusement park in Seal Beach—the Joy Zone. Stanton had imported the manager of the 1915 Pan-Pacific Exhibition in San Francisco and many of its attractions, including the roller coaster and the Scintillators light show. (The fact that I.W. Hellman was one of the San Francisco exhibition's largest financial backers probably made the acquisition easier.)

Sometimes you could see the daredevil aerial acrobatics of Joe Boquel, bathing beauty contests filmed by Mack Sennett's Keystone Studios or a Fatty Arbuckle comedy filmed for the Balboa Studios, located in Long Beach at Sixth and Alamitos Avenue. From 1915 to 1919, Balboa was one of the largest motion picture production facilities in the country. With a huge back lot at Signal Hill, Balboa was larger than the Hollywood studios. A couple of films were even filmed in Los Alamitos, one of the most notable being *Band of Blood* starring former outlaw turned movie star Al Jennings.

On July 28, 1921, oil was discovered on Signal Hill by a Shell Oil team led by geologist Dwight Thornburg, whose father, Charles, once managed the Alamitos rancho. Within weeks, hundreds of derricks dotted the hillside. The oil field, the richest in the United States, made the Balboa Studio's back lot too valuable to keep as a production site. The growing smell and smoky air made the main studio far less desirable as well. The Balboa Company sold off its props to studios in Hollywood, which now became the undisputed capital of motion picture production.

Other oil discoveries were made all along the Newport–Inglewood fault, making millionaires of Fred Bixby and numerous lucky landowners in Huntington Beach and adding to the wealth of the heirs of I.W. Hellman and the members of the Bolsa Chica Gun Club. For the Bixby Land Company heirs, it was not so good. They had subdivided and sold most of their valuable Signal Hill property, and what they still owned produced some, but not spectacular, amounts of oil. Shell Oil even drilled for oil on Bixby Land Company property in Los Alamitos, sinking a well in 1922 near Chestnut and Katella, but it too came up dry. Los Alamitos dairyman Louis Denni, who had bought a big lot atop Signal Hill to build his home, struck it rich when oil was discovered under his new house. He would sell his Los Alamitos dairy operations to "Mac" McOmie and take much of his new money to found the Wilmington Savings and Loan Company.

All the drilling activity in the area brought in a new labor force—oil drillers and laborers, many of whom moved to a new Los Alamitos tract called City Garden Acres (present-day Apartment Row, south of Katella). Developed in mid-1924 on land owned by Jacob Sterns & Sons (a Los Angeles landowner), the six-hundred-acre tract sold half-acre farm lots that were promoted by barber turned real estate salesman Rush Green as "big enough to raise chickens." Green's daughter Lura, who was twelve when the family moved from Long Beach into the still not open tract in 1923, remembered that "sugar beets were still growing all around. "We used to get the leaves and have them for dinner like spinach. They were real sweet and real good. We'd go out and get the young ones."

After subdividing the sections and laying out streets, Rush Green set up a demonstration house on one of the lots near Katella—to show "what could be done with a quarter acre and chickens and rabbits."

One of the first set of lots was bought on July 18, 1924, by Robert and Hazel Campbell, near Maple and Farquhar. Other early landowners were John and Jane Sjostrom, who purchased land on Howard, just in from Los Alamitos Boulevard. The tract "south of town" grew so fast that the September 26, 1924 *Press-Telegram* reported that Laurel School "may have to hire an additional teacher and hold classes in the auditorium."

Soon, the former beet fields were making way for new homes. By early 1925, City Garden Acres had grown at such a pace that Rush Green was promoting the tract as a separate community, with newspaper articles lauding such improvements as the "new two-story brick building with the ground floor for stores, and the upper floor for a Community Hall," and the new baseball diamond and grandstand at Farquhar and Los Alamitos Boulevard where "the Los Alamitos baseball team will play under the City Garden Acres colors." By the end of the year, the *Press-Telegram* listed Los Alamitos and City Garden Acres as two separate suburbs.

Whether one town or two, the new residents gave new life to the town. Many of the newcomers joined the Women's Improvement Club, which raised money for a stop sign at Los Alamitos and Cerritos and new curbs

A Brief History of Los Alamitos and Rossmoor

In 1924, barber turned realtor Rush Green opened the City Garden Acres tract south of Katella, marketing it as half-acre farm lots where you could even raise chickens. Among the first buyers were Robert and Hazel Campbell, who constructed the home pictured above at the corner of Maple and Farquhar. By 1926, the tract had become so popular that Green was touting City Garden Acres as a separate community, with its own civic building and baseball field where "the Los Alamitos baseball team would play this season under the City Garden Acres colors."

around the church and hosted dances at the Sugar Company clubhouse, with as many as one hundred dancers in attendance enjoying the vocals of Theodore Arbeely, accompanied by Miss Evelyn Montgomery on the piano.

In mid-1927, a new newspaper, the *Los Alamitos Press*, made its debut in the community, with Frank Jones as its editor. In August, Jones joined with the editors of four other young publications, the *Cypress Enterprise*, *Stanton Progress*, *Midway City–Westminster Gazette* and the more established *Buena Park News* ("roots back to 1923"), to form the West Orange County Publishing Company. Henry Schmitz, publisher of the Buena Park paper, was chosen to head the new operation's business affairs, and Jones was the advertising manager. The *Enterprise*'s Worth Cuthbert Miller became managing editor of all the papers, which had a combined circulation of 2,800. W.C. Miller was well suited and knowledgeable about the

Oil, Sugar Blues, Horse Meat and Earthquakes

The first Mexicans in the Los Alamitos area were temporary field workers, but by 1910 they composed about one-quarter of the town's permanent population. Paula Torres came to Los Alamitos as a teenager when her father worked the sugar beet fields. In 1926, she married Louis Cano, who operated a billiard parlor on Main (now Reagan) Street. Paula soon opened a store just down the street that is still remembered by old-timers for its candy selection. Known as "Paulita," she was a fixture in the community until her death in October 1999 at the age of one hundred.

community. His father, George, was one of Cypress's earliest and most influential dairymen. By 1930, David Stocks was editor of the *Los Alamitos Press*. In 1931, Schmitz sold out his interest to W.C. Miller, who later split off the papers, keeping only the Buena Park, Cypress and Los Alamitos publications. But by the end of World War II, only the Buena Park paper had survived.

The growing population of Belgians, combined with the existing large number of Mexican residents and the significant number of Irish (O'Connor, Reagan, Feaghan, Malloy, et cetera) and French (Labourdette) background, resulted in a large Catholic population who wanted a church of their own. The mission parish of St. Isadore was established in 1921 to serve not only Los Alamitos but also Stanton, Garden Grove,

A Brief History of Los Alamitos and Rossmoor

Westminster and the *colonias* (barrios) of Independencia and Manzanillo. Not having a building, the parishioners met at times at the Harmona Hotel, in some of the stores and occasionally in the Congregational Church building. (Many other churches also met in this building in the early days. The 1897 Bixby flyers call the building a Union Church, a common term for a building that housed multiple denominations.)

On August 21, 1924, the Bixby Land Company granted the Los Angeles and Monterey Diocese a lot for a new parish church at the corner of Reagan and Alvarado, adjacent to the Congregational/Union Church building. Someone paid the ten-dollar filing fee, and the grant deed spelled the parish as "St. Isidore." The two spellings were used almost interchangeably until the mid- to late 1950s, when the "i" finally permanently trumped the "a."

The original St. Isidore chapel, a simple brick building, was completed as early as March 1926, when the *Press-Telegram* mentioned a service at the church. With two churches now on the street, Alvarado Avenue was called Church Street on some maps, but the street soon became better known for the ranch and school that were at the Anaheim end of the long dirt road, where walnut grower John Rea named his ranch after his two daughters, Kate and Ella. By 1934, a small elementary school and the road had also taken the name Katella.

Local farmers were impacted by the outbreak in April 1924 of the highly contagious hoof-and-mouth disease in Los Angeles County near Cudahy and Downey. Area agricultural officials quarantined cattle and humans (who could transmit the malady through their persons or luggage). Arizona officials quarantined travelers from California until they were disinfected. Orange County posted armed guards at the Los Angeles county line with orders to shoot. Despite the precautions, symptoms were found in the Thompson and Main herd of 203 dairy cattle in Los Alamitos at Spring (Cerritos) and Bloomfield. To prevent a "possible spread of the disease, officials with the Citizens Emergency Committee even tried to track down two Mexican workers—milkers—who had left the Alamitos farm to find work elsewhere. One, who had boarded a train for Calexico, was found by Imperial County authorities and was thoroughly disinfected before being allowed to continue on his way. The other was thought to be in the Long Beach area, trying to find work on another dairy ranch. But it was too late, and government workers slaughtered the Thomson and Main herd and the herds of other local dairies, including those of Louis Denni and the Bixby Land Company. The cattle were buried in long ditches dug to hold the carcasses.

H.E. Thompson gave up dairy farming and took up real estate. (His sign is still in the Los Alamitos Museum). His wife wrote an article for the *LA Times*, telling about their rural home—"two acres, 194 fruit trees of fifty varieties, and eighty seven vines of twelve kinds…tucked back of fourteen large palms that extended across the street front of the place."

Some of the Los Alamitos dairies restocked and resumed operations. Long Beach and other cities passed laws outlawing dairy and hog farms and set deadlines for those operations to relocate. Many ended up moving to the areas around Cypress and Artesia.

By 1925, Hamilton moved on, and Strodthoff became the factory manager. Bennis was his number two man. He was qualified and by now was also Strodthoff's brother-in-law. Both had married daughters of town merchant George Watts (who shows up in the 1900 census as the town's "barber").

Younger daughter Una married Strodthoff and became a leading lady in Los Alamitos, serving on many groups, including the Women's Improvement Association. Older sister Nina married Bennis and apparently led a very active social life. The *Press-Telegram* mentioned dinners in Los Angeles and horseback rides with other Long Beach ladies of society. Nina showed excellent handwriting as the census taker in 1930. But within a couple years Karl had moved to Temecula, and Nina partnered with Jim Arnerich to build the Glide'er Inn, the landmark restaurant across from Crawford Field, the old Seal Beach airport located on the northeast corner of the Pacific Coast Highway and Bay Road (now Seal Beach Boulevard).

The nematode pest is often blamed for ending the sugar beet industry in Los Alamitos, but this is only partly true, as crop rotation minimized the worm's impact. Far more significant were the end of protective tariffs, increased foreign competition, higher labor costs and the greater profitability of other crops, especially lima beans. While Orange County dropped from processing around 50,000 acres of beets per year in 1913 to just 12,000 acres in 1926, the Los Alamitos Company's output dropped only slightly. It still grew the most beets in Orange County (over 6,500 acres in 1926), but it became more economical to ship those beets to a single factory for processing.

In early 1926, after twenty-nine straight seasons, Strodthoff shut down the Los Alamitos factory, and he and the Los Alamitos crew assumed much of the management of the area's largest, best-equipped factory: the Holly Company's Santa Ana factory off Dyer Road.

By now a new generation was assuming control of the area. First, in early 1917, Jotham Bixby died, leaving the Bixby Land Company in some disarray. His son, George, became the president, but some personal scandals had left him an ineffective leader. George died in 1922 and was succeded by Lewellyn's son, Llewellyn (beginning with two "l's"), who would run the company for the next twenty-two years and guide it skillfully through some very difficult times.

In March 1925, William A. Clark died in New York City (leaving an estate worth about $600 million in 2010 dollars). In September 1926, J. Ross Clark passed away in Los Angeles. Stock for the Clark operations—including the United Verde Mine, the Los Alamitos Sugar Company, the Montana Land Company and the Clark & Montana Realty Company—was distributed to numerous family members, including William A. Clark Jr., who would use part of it to fund the Los Angeles Philharmonic Orchestra, the Hollywood Bowl and the William A. Clark Library of rare books and manuscripts, which he donated to UCLA in 1934.

Nephew Clark Joaquin Bonner, who owned an insurance company in Los Angeles, assumed management of the Montana Ranch while Strodthoff continued to manage the sugar-related operations. Bonner accelerated the company's transition from agriculture to industry and pursued large companies like Ford, Chrysler and Consolidated Aircraft to build plants on company land in Los Alamitos and by the Long Beach Airport. The 1929 stock market crash ended those ambitions, as well as a deal with the Janss Company, the builders of Westwood Village and Thousand Oaks, to develop a new community centered on Bouton Lake, the bubbling artesian well that had once attracted sightseers by sending water over fifty feet into the air but in recent years had been used by the Cerritos Gun Club. Undaunted, the Montana Land Company self-financed the development of Lakewood Village and a country club designed by William P. Bell (co-designer of courses at the Bel-Air, Riviera, Virginia and Los Angeles Country Clubs) and paved a 110-foot-wide section of Carson Boulevard from Cherry Avenue to Lincoln Avenue in Orange County, completing one of the last links in one of the earliest transcontinental highways.

In early 1927, the mighty Babe Ruth briefly came to Los Alamitos. Fresh off an outstanding 1926 baseball season, the Bambino's nationwide tour took him to Long Beach's State Theater. During his one-week stint, he accepted the invitation of Long Beach auto dealer Glenn E. Thomas to go duck hunting at the Farmers Gun Club a mile east of the sugar factory. The January 23, 1927 issue of the *Press-Telegram* reports that he bagged his quota of twenty-four ducks and returned to do his afternoon show.

Earlier that same month, Los Alamitos merchants and businessmen formed the Los Alamitos Chamber of Commerce. Although the sugar company had moved its processing to Santa Ana, the local businessmen were optimistic. The part-time factory and its obnoxious smells were gone. They were next to Long Beach, touted as "the fastest-growing city in the United States." Opportunities existed with the right leadership and an active chamber. Longtime merchant and postmaster Hugh T. O'Connor and W.C. Crofoot headed this organization for most of the next fifteen years, and realtor Rush Green would play an active role, as would his daughter Lura and her husband, August Labourdette. Loren Cloud would succeed O'Connor as the town's postmaster and become chamber president in 1941. The chamber worked hard to market and improve the west Orange County and coast areas. It sponsored home- and business-decorating contests, backed flood control projects and got bus companies to run their routes to Anaheim through Los Alamitos. In 1933, it even backed an unsuccessful plan to build a horse racetrack near present Seal Beach Boulevard and Westminster Avenue.

More women joined the Women's Improvement Association and the Willing Worker Club, as well. Some of the local women also belonged to the Women's Club of Artesia. They met in the old sugar factory clubhouse. Bessie Juskjievicz recalled, "We were the smallest federated club in Orange County and had the largest clubhouse."

Many of these same ladies succeeded in 1935 to get an independent branch of the Orange County library opened in town, with Grace Green as the librarian. Previously, it had been part of Laurel School.

Many former sugar factory workers found work at the recovering local dairy farms where farmers like William "Mac" McOmie paid them seventy-five dollars a month but with only two days off. Not surprisingly, such conditions drew the attention of labor unions. In April 1936, on a Sunday morning at 1:00 a.m., five milkers out of nine employed at the McOmie Ranch refused to work unless they were paid ninety dollars a month with four days off. A neighbor furnished McOmie with the necessary help, and the string was milked on time. But on the way home, the neighbor was reportedly beaten by the five striking milkers. Strikers affiliated with the Mexican Agricultural Workers Union of Los Alamitos

Floods continued to be a recurring problem in the area. In 1936, the waters again reached up to the first floors of the stores on Los Alamitos Boulevard, including Jack Sjostrom's Gas Station and Watts Groceries on the northeast corner of Los Alamitos and Florista, where the VCA Rossmoor–El Dorado Animal Hospital is now located.

Oil, Sugar Blues, Horse Meat and Earthquakes

In 1936, Robert and Hazel Campbell opened their own grocery store on Los Alamitos Boulevard a few buildings north of the Watts store. In the photo, Hazel and Robert pose in front of their good selection of produce and canned goods. In 1946, when their son, Bobby, and son-in-law, Harlan Hubert, returned from World War II, Campbell's moved across the street to a new store at the corner of Los Alamitos and Florista (where Sunrise Glass is now located).

and the Congress of Industrial Organizations (CIO), began picketing the dairy, despite an anti-picketing ordinance in Orange County. The Mexican Agricultural Workers Union, which had its local offices in the Valencia Hotel on Pine Street, also supported Harry Bridges and his International Longshoremen's Union when they tried to organize farm workers around the state.

Nature also treated Los Alamitos roughly. While the floods were expected, technology made some of them far worse. In the late 1920s, the rapidly spreading floodwater loosened one of the tanks at the new Texaco Oil Tank farm at Ball and Denni, and oil started making its way through Los Alamitos toward the ocean. Lura Labourdette remembers the floodwaters coming through City Garden Acres, the oil sometimes carrying large batches of straw. The chickens at the demonstration house and the surrounding homes would seek refuge on the straw, "not knowing the straw was just floating on top of the oil. They'd just jump down on it, [sink] and come up with oil all over them…The poor chickens didn't have a chance…That was a pretty tough one."

Bessie Juskievicz remembers the factory sending workers "with hoses and brooms to sweep the oil off the lawn and the water as it was going down. But for years when the children played in the back yard they had to take their shoes off at the back door because they had oil on the shoes because it was buried in the grass."

On Friday, May 10, 1933, at 5:54 p.m., a 6.4-magnitude earthquake struck the Long Beach area. Lura Labourdette remembered, "We thought it was an explosion. Everybody ran outside." Angelita Reyes Sisneros recalled that it was Lent, and her family was getting ready to go to a Friday evening service at St. Isidore's. She was holding her baby sister when the quake began. "The floor was moving all over, and it was hard to move. Everybody finally got outside—we didn't dare stay in the house—and we slept outdoors that night. Everybody did."

The first shake lasted eleven seconds. At St. Isidore's, loosened bricks reportedly fell on a priest preparing for Mass. Paulita Cano, the owner of a market on Reagan Street—with the best candy counter in town, by some reports—was in the church at the time and remembers being up to her knees in debris.

Bessie Juskjievicz says their family was just sitting down for dinner. "I had a big white bass in the oven when the earthquake hit. My fish came out of the oven onto the floor." A baby grand piano in the den went across the room and cut off her brand-new curtains she had purchased only a week before.

The second shock struck at 6:06 p.m., then others came at 6:10, 6:12 and 6:15 p.m. There would be thirty-one aftershocks by midnight.

Jesus Torres remembers that a fissure opened on Los Alamitos Boulevard, and there was concern that some of the cars filled with "refugees" from Long Beach might fall in the openings. A lantern was brought out to mark the fissure. That proved to be more problematic, as the fissure had created a gas leak that had to be dealt with.

Oil, Sugar Blues, Horse Meat and Earthquakes

At the sugar factory, Bessie Juskievicz joined her husband for a quick inspection. "The entire south wall of the clubhouse had fallen out. You could see the bedrooms upstairs and the kitchen and the dining room below."

Later that night, the Juskjieviczs drove over to the Montana Ranch "and sat on the ground. The ranch manager had a big fire going, we all sat. The earth would shake, and I was just sure it was going to crack and we would fall down in it. I was just petrified." After a while, the family decided to return to Los Alamitos via Carson Avenue and Hawaiian Gardens. At the bridge by Ball Road, the police blocked their way, saying there was going to be a tidal wave. Bruno drove over to Bloomfield and then to Cerritos to return to their house, gather their belongings and "Cokes and things" and then drive up to Brea Canyon, where they spent the night.

Others went to Marina Hill near Seal Beach or Signal Hill. Reyes remembers one gas station owner in Los Alamitos told the people they could take his gas, he was going to high ground. The Labourdettes loaded up their car and went to the Whittier hills, but after a few hours they went to some friend's in Stanton who had "pitched a tent out back" and spent the night. Most came back, but some, like Fred Avila's family, moved right then to Palm Springs in the Coachella Valley and never returned.

Juskievicz remembers how the townspeople set up a commissary and that the Red Cross brought cans of milk and corned beef for the quake victims. Sadly, one of the town's damaged structures was the historic Harmona Hotel. Reports differ as to the extent of the damage to the old building, but apparently it was bad enough that the owners didn't want to spend money to repair it. By early 1936, James Watts had purchased the building, and after removing part of the roof and porch coverings, he moved the two-story structure to Los Alamitos Boulevard, just north of Florista and Jack Sjostrom's Gilmore Gas Station. Watts used the downstairs for his grocery store, while his family lived upstairs in one unit and rented out at least two others. But overall, Los Alamitos was fortunate, suffering only $25,000 worth of damage, a fraction of what other nearby towns suffered. At the Labourdette winery, an old artesian well that had sanded up was shaken enough by the quake to start producing water again.

But overall Los Al was fortunate, suffering only an estimated $25,000 in damage, a fraction of the damage to many neighboring communities.

The town recovered. Richard Longeval, who had converted his blacksmith shop to a gas station in 1931, continued to sell gas at his corner lot—Standard Oil and Mobil brand.

Ironically, the Texaco company opened up a small processing facility adjacent to this, near the oil pipelines that ran from the Texaco tank farm (constructed in 1929) at Ball and Denni through an easement along Coyote Creek. By 1940, Pathfinder Oil had also opened a small refinery to the west.

Hugh O'Connor bought some more lots around town that he rented out, but he kept working in his store and acting as the town's postmaster and unofficial arithmetic teacher. Leon Sjostrom, then a young schoolboy, remembers that whenever he'd go into O'Connor's store to buy candy, the old man wouldn't let him have the item until he could answer an arithmetic problem. By 1940, O'Connor had retired. The effect on the town's arithmetic scores was unreported.

The sugar factory buildings did not remain idle for long. Dr. A.A. Gilliuame leased the old clubhouse and converted it into a sanitarium, a facility offering long-term medical care. A lumber company leased the old machine shop and used the area where the beet sheds once stood. And by 1935, the town's biggest employer was the pet food factory operated by veterinarian William J. Ross. In 1932, Ross, originally from Santa Monica, leased the sugar factory's main buildings and moved his dog and cat food manufacturing operation from Norwalk to Los Alamitos. Fred Bixby and others objected to Ross's methods for obtaining meat product—contracting with Nevada and Arizona Indian tribes to catch wild mustangs and packing them like sardines into trailers to be hauled across the Mojave Desert. Many animals died en route. Ross and his nephew Fred, the company manager, were accused of animal cruelty but were eventually acquitted. Ross also purchased three fishing ships— one being the former yacht of the king of Spain—to get seafood for his product. The director of the San Diego Museum of Natural History wrote articles detailing the slaughter of sea lions, and the United States urged Mexico to deny Ross a fishing permit.

Oil, Sugar Blues, Horse Meat and Earthquakes

In 1932, Dr. William Ross, a veterinarian turned pet food manufacturer, leased the main sugar factory building and warehouse to produce his dog and cat food. Ross was sued by Fred Bixby and others who didn't approve of his source of meat: wild mustangs caught by Indian tribes in Utah and Arizona and endangered sea lions caught off Mexico. Ross survived for awhile thanks to extensive advertising (like this newspaper ad above with Oscar-winning actress Merle Oberon) and extensive promotion (top-notch semi-pro baseball teams and floats in the Rose Parade) but continued opposition, the economy and shortages caused by the war proved too much to overcome. Ross filed for bankruptcy in 1942 and his brand and machinery were sold at auction. A Tennessee doctor bought the brand and took it to bigger heights in the 1950s and early 1960s, but by then the business had relocated to Vernon.

"TO BE SURE I FEED MY DOGS Dr. Ross' DOG FOOD" *says* Merle Oberon STAR OF THE SAMUEL GOLDWYN PRODUCTION "DARK ANGEL"

★ Here is shown Miss Oberon feeding her pedigreed Dalmatian dogs—popularly known as coach dogs back in the horse and buggy era. In Hollywood, where some of the world's finest dogs are owned by motion picture stars, it is only natural that Dr. Ross' dog food is such an outstanding favorite.

At all Grocers' and Pet Shops

This scientifically prepared food contains exactly the right proportions of pure, lean meat and other ingredients for a perfectly balanced ration — supplying the complete nutritional requirements of your dog or cat. To be sure—insist on Dr. Ross Dog and Cat Food.

PACKED BY DR. W. J. ROSS CO.   LOS ANGELES CALIFORNIA

But Ross survived this as well, and the 1940 census shows that the company employed many of the town's residents. To promote and advertise his product, Ross used Hollywood stars like Oscar-winning actress Merle Oberon; sponsored top-level semipro baseball teams; and entered floats in the Rose Parade. But by 1942, he was bankrupt, and the company's equipment was sold at an auction at the factory. The "Dr. Ross" brand was bought by a Tennessee businessman who re-energized it in the 1950s with a catchy jingle that was played repeatedly on television, especially during children's programming. But that was long after it had moved out of Los Alamitos. As for Ross, things did not get better for him. He died in Long Beach in 1964, an indigent.

8
THE BASE

In 1938, even before the war in Europe and the Japanese attack on Pearl Harbor, the U.S. Congress had authorized the construction of new naval aviation training facilities, and U.S. Navy leaders began looking around for new flat spots for their air bases. Los Alamitos's wide-open and flat farmland did not escape their attention.

Because of his oil income, Fred Bixby had neither the need nor inclination to sell off any of his beloved ranch. Others, including his sister, Susannah Bixby Bryant, were not so reluctant.

A two-paragraph item in the February 25, 1941 *LA Times* reported that the Naval Reserve Air Base (NRAB) in Long Beach would move to a new four-hundred-acre field in the vicinity of Los Alamitos.

On March 29, 1941, the *Press-Telegram* reported that the Navy had bought from Mrs. Susannah Bixby Bryant 1,300 acres of open farmland for "a huge new reserve base for Navy aviation." This was immediately south of the previously purchased land. The next day, the *Times* announced construction would begin on a 965-acre site, adjoining 480.6 acres already leased from the Los Alamitos Sugar Company, "in the form of a square , adjoining the Los Alamitos town site, and extends north and south of Katella Road." (This would be the property south of the tracks between Lexington and Walker—land now occupied by Cottonwood Church, the racetrack, Costco and the Carrier Row sections of Los Alamitos.) Then the reports get confusing.

A Brief History of Los Alamitos and Rossmoor

Local old-timers remember Navy pilots practicing touch-and-go landings on this site, which would make it the first military airbase in Orange County, a fact further confirmed by the April 3, 1941 *Press-Telegram*, which reported work was to start on a 480-acre site, adding that the reserve unit was already using a 160-acre runway leased from the Sugar Company.

Court documents filed on March 28, 1941, show the U.S. Navy originally purchased 475.16 acres from Susannah Bixby Bryant. The land was a mile wide and ran three-quarters of a mile. During construction, and perhaps after the attack on Pearl Harbor, the Navy decided it needed to expand the new base by a quarter mile on each side and began additional condemnations. On May 6, 1942, thirteen property transfers were filed with Orange County. The transfer involved five owners—two parcels from the Los Alamitos Sugar Company (118.2 acres, the bottom third of what had been previously leased), one from the Artesian Land Company (79.4 acres), two more smaller parcels from Susannah Bixby Bryant (80 acres total), three from her brother Fred Bixby (240 acres) and two from Jacob Sterns and sons (118.2 acres).

The documents also list that the tenant farmers had to be evicted—including four Belgians leasing Bixby lands (Louis Schiettecatte, L. Lerno, Jules DePauw and Frank Watte).

Newspapers at the time said the price was undisclosed, but later base histories say the Navy offered Mrs. Bixby $350.00 an acre, but that in the best patriotic spirit she sold it for $300.00. However, court records show Susannah Bixby Bryant was paid $227.00 per acre for the first 1941 purchase, and then she and all the other landowners were compensated at $220.50 per acre on the subsequent 1942 transfer. This is not a bad price considering that a little farther south, James Irvine reportedly received only $100.00 an acre for the Santa Ana, Tustin and El Toro air bases.

Whether either Bixby was an enthusiastic partner in these land swaps is unknown, but Fred was definitely not a willing partner on a subsequent military land grab. A few months later, he was fighting tooth and nail to keep the Navy from taking eighty-eight acres of his prime Long Beach mesa farmland for a new hospital (the one currently located at Seventh and Bellflower). Bixby announced that "he will make every effort to halt

The Base

the threatened condemnation of the area" and tried to enlist friends on the chamber of commerce to help him fight this takeover of some of his best bean fields. His friends said he would get so frustrated when talking about it that he was almost in tears.

Not surprisingly, the Navy got its way, and construction funds for the new airbase and hospital soon followed. Congress authorized over $3 million for the air facility, which would have two runways, one 5,000 feet (fifteen city blocks), and the other 3,500 feet. Half of the money was to go toward housing facilities, hangars, shops and administration buildings. The buildings at Los Alamitos and the Roosevelt Navy Base at the Port of Long Beach were designed by well-known architects Paul Revere Williams and A. Quincy Jones. The pair's art deco moderne style, especially at the Roosevelt Navy Base, is considered some of the finest examples of publicly funded art deco work. Jones's work on the original hangar and control tower also displayed some sleek art deco touches, until it was rather insensitively altered during some later "improvements."

The Belgian tenant farmers who had been working these lands now had to find new sections to work, and over the next couple months much became available.

Within hours of the December 7, 1941 attack on Pearl Harbor, U.S. government officials began arresting local Japanese nationals and leaders. By February 1942, over nineteen thousand Japanese-Americans from Los Angeles and Orange County had been removed from Southern California.

The Japanese resettlement was just one result of the near hysteria in Southern California immediately after Pearl Harbor. After submarine-launched Japanese airplanes attacked a Santa Barbara refinery, the West Coast was blacked out at night. Automobiles were driven only with parking lights or taped headlights. Large antiaircraft batteries and searchlights were placed at the new local bases, as well as the Bolsa Chica Gun Club and near Cypress and other towns, where sailors and soldiers from Fort MacArthur in San Pedro and newly recruited civilian air wardens kept a vigilant eye on the shore and air.

Local civilians had to make sacrifices as the government quickly set up ration boards for items such as meat, gasoline and even sugar. The Seal Beach board also covered Los Alamitos, Midway City, Barber City and Westminster. Locals, including restaurants like the Glide'er Inn and defense workers living in Seal Beach and Los Alamitos, asked the local board to do something about the paltry six-ounce-weekly ration of meat they got in mid-1943.

Within a month of Pearl Harbor, the Navy began expansion from 5,200 aircraft to 27,500 aircraft, and NAS Los Alamitos would train many of the pilots who would man those aircraft.

Los Alamitos would be an E-base (Elimination Base), where cadets endured tough drills and weaker, less-qualified future pilots washed out. With the base still under construction, the first cadets roomed in area boardinghouses with little supervision, and curfew was on the honor system. Some stayed at the YMCA, and others stayed with Los Alamitos residents with available rooms. With her daughters away at UCLA, Bessie Juskievicz agreed to take in two cadets. She ended up "adopting more or less two boys from Memphis, Tennessee" and became lifelong friends. But life with the locals (and without bed checks) came to an end near the end of May 1942, when the expanded facilities at NAS Los Alamitos welcomed its first class of five hundred aviation cadets. By July 1, the NRAB Long Beach command reported that it was now calling

When it first opened, the Los Alamitos Air Base was a Reserve Elimination base, where cadets were put through tough training and testing, and many were eliminated. Cadets spent half the time in a classroom and the other half learning how to fly in a Stearman biplane. Because of the color they were painted, they were called the "Yellow Peril."

The Base

itself NRAB Los Alamitos, that all flight equipment had been moved and that "all flight activities were being carried out at the new location."

The cadets were paid twenty-one dollars per month as seamen second class. They learned to fly in plywood Boeing Stearman N2T1s biplanes, all painted yellow and called, naturally, the Yellow Peril. They studied for seven hours a day. In the classroom they learned Morse code, dead reckoning, celestial navigation and rate of closure; in the plane, they practiced takeoffs and landings and basic maneuvers at Los Alamitos and

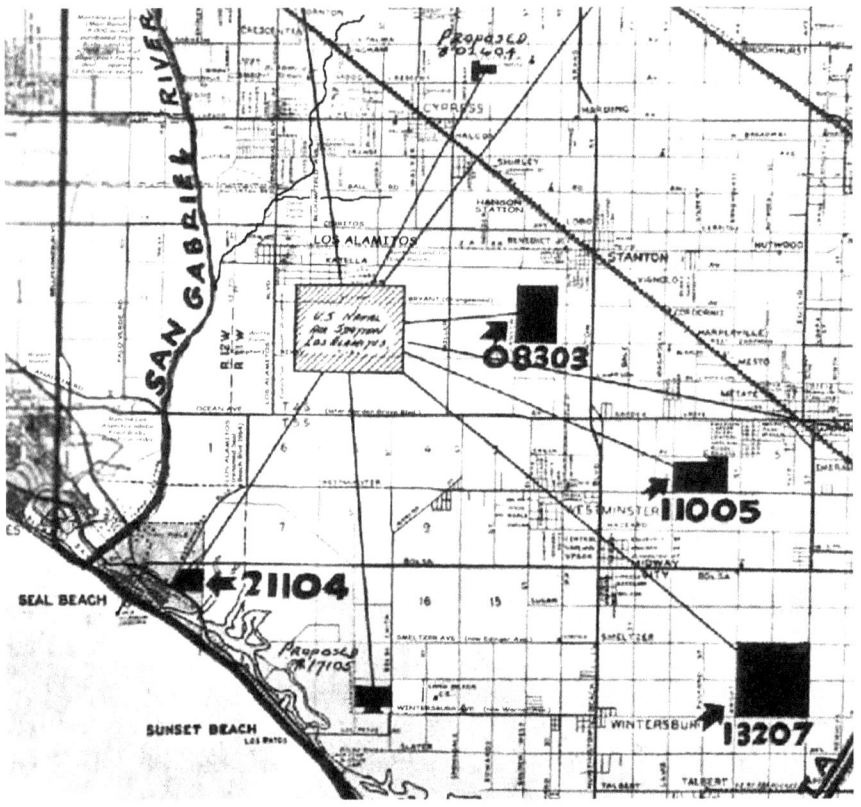

Los Alamitos was the center of a network of naval outlying airfields (NOLFs) purchased or leased by the navy to allow pilots training at Los Al (and later El Toro) to practice landings throughout the Orange County area. Among the NOLFs were Mile Square (13207, Fountain Valley), Anaheim (Leubeken), Fullerton, Norwalk, East Long Beach/Bolsa Chica (17105, now Meadowlark Golf Course, Huntington Beach), Crawford Field (21104, Seal Beach), the Horse Farm (08305, Stanton), Haster Farm (11005, Garden Grove) and Palisades (now Eastbluff area in Newport Beach). Most of the outlying airfields eventually became parks, school sites or golf courses.

the surrounding auxiliary airfields, which included Crawford Field (Seal Beach), East Long Beach (now Meadowlark Golf Course in Huntington Beach), Mile Square in Fountain Valley, Eastbluff Park in Newport Beach and others in Stanton, Garden Grove and Anaheim.

Accidents inevitably happened. Some planes nosed over on ground loops; others touched down too near the end of the runway, hit a dike and nosed over into one of the base's treatment ponds. One cadet cut his landing low and short and came away with corn from the adjoining farmland on his tail. The close call shook him up, and he turned in his cadet's wings. Others were not so lucky. One cadet was killed after his plane collided with another cadet plane and then fell hundreds of feet onto the roof of a base supply building.

But by the end of 1942, Los Al had graduated 729 pilots who were then sent to Corpus Christi, Texas, for more specialized training.

By early 1943, the facility had increased its planes from 36 to 140. There was now a pool and a gymnasium, handball courts and a base theater that would show movies and be used for many USO shows. Since the base was one of the closest to Hollywood, Bob Hope frequently performed his weekly radio shows there, trying out new material, sometimes using invented names like the "Seal Beach Refueling Depot" to avoid always saying the show was from Los Alamitos.

The new theater wasn't the only venue for entertainment. Some cadets were invited to escort candidates at the Miss California pageant held in Long Beach.

The station's sports teams, like the Los Alamitos Air Raiders football team—manned by many pro and college All-American athletes—played local colleges before beginning their service conference schedule. The Los Al baseball team, managed by Billy Feisner, fielded a roster that included pitchers George (Jasper) Caster of the St. Louis Browns, Vern Olson (Chicago Cubs) and catcher Cliff Dapper, Jack Graham and pitcher Jack Paepke, all of whom spent time with the Dodgers in 1942. The roster also included many players from Long Beach, including future Hall of Famer Bob Lemon, who attended Los Alamitos's Laurel School for a few years in the late 1920s and was now only a few years out of Wilson High.

The Base

The Los Al station baseball team not only played in a Long Beach Recreation League but also in the California Winter League, which featured the first known instances of black teams playing against whites in an integrated baseball league. Two black professional teams, the Philadelphia Royal Giants and the Elite Giants, played with the local white teams in that league.

On December 31, 1942, the UCLA Bruins basketball team, led by Dick West's twenty-three points, scored an easy 68–43 win over the Los Alamitos's "Air Base Team," whose box score lists the following players: Teach, 7; Winters, 12; Mears, 2; White, 11; Herron, 5; Behrens, 3; and Berry, 3.

But the base's main mission was to help win a war. By January 1943, NAS Los Alamitos had been "upgraded" to full Naval Air Station status, and in August it became a Carrier Air Support Unit. The facility and its 140 planes now provided training and support for carrier-based aviation units in the Pacific Ocean—on the USS *Langley*, USS *Saratoga*, USS *Essex* and USS *Lexington*.

The most storied unit to come out of Los Al during World War II was Air Group 19, a wing of fighters, bombers and torpedo (nicknamed "torpeckers") squadrons that was officially commissioned in August 1943. Led first by Carl Jung and then by Lieutenant Commander Hugh Winters, a Silver Star winner in the North African campaign, Fighting Squadron Nineteen would distinguish itself in some of the legendary naval air battles of the Pacific War.

The group trained for six months in Los Alamitos, honing individual and group tactics during the day. The base chaplain, C. Pardee Erdman, provided great value beyond his theological skills. As the former college roommate of Assistant Secretary of the Navy James Forrestal, Erdman cut through red tape to get good planes for training. He was also a professor at Occidental College, a resident of posh San Marino and a golfing buddy of Bob Hope and Bing Crosby. He not only introduced the pilots to the best golf courses in the area, but he also introduced them to the world of Hollywood stars and starlets, arranged for the pilots to attend shows in Hollywood and helped the stars to do radio shows from the base.

A Brief History of Los Alamitos and Rossmoor

Air Group 19 had a larger than normal share of seasoned fliers, one being Howard "Redbird" Burnette, a pilot cut from the same cloth as Douglas Fairbanks or Errol Flynn. As a dive bomber pilot, he had earned a Navy Air Medal in the Battle of Coral Sea, prompting the Navy to use the handsome Burnette for stateside recruiting trips. Burnette made the switch to fighters, and while retraining at Los Alamitos, the Navy let him travel up to Hollywood to appear on the Ginny Simms radio show in early January 1944, much to the delight of his hometown of Coldwater, Kansas.

The fighters trained with the F6F Hellcat, loving its response, its power and its six fifty-caliber machine guns and the two hundred pounds of armor plate on their backseat, which protected pilots from the bullets fired by pursuing planes. The fighters had three roles. First was to fly escort to ensure the two-man bombers and three-man torpedo planes could sink carriers, battleships and cruisers. During escort, no fighters could veer off to undertake attacks on their own. Their second role was to fly CAP, combat air patrol, over the task force. During this, they were free to attack incoming enemy aircraft. Third was to scout—to fly out to assigned sectors in coordinated fashion and try to find the enemy's task force.

The Bombers trained on the Douglas Dauntless bomber, a reliable but slow plane that would soon be replaced.

For most of the week, the squadrons did their own training, fighters shooting at towed targets and bombers practicing dives on oil slicks and barges off Huntington Beach and doing bounce drills (simulated carrier landings on marked-off areas of the Los Alamitos runway).

Once a week, they had a coordinated exercise—"group gropes" with the torpedo planes hovering below the bombers while the Hellcats provided overhead cover as they "attacked" a target at sea, usually a Navy ship going up and down the coast. No one flew straight at his target, making it easy for enemy guns to line up their sights. Nearing their target, the group's pilots veered off from formation and came in at a target in helix-like spirals.

Night landings were practiced on dark fields to simulate aircraft carriers. Even experienced pilots flew through the surrounding trees during a pre-dawn takeoff or clipped power lines running around the edge of the base.

Not all were lucky. A VB-19 ordnance ground crewman was dragged to death when his foot caught in a gunnery target tow line as it was being lifted off by a fighter. In November 1943, a pilot and gunner were killed when they hit the water off Huntington Beach after failing to pull out of a dive. The glassy water gave little indication of height. Noted another pilot, somberly, "We decided that planes can kill, and you need to keep your mind on business."

But human nature being what it is, the intense training required a balance.

Chaplain Erdman introduced Winters and some other pilots to his "best friends," who "owned the Bolsa Chica Gun Club, and extended the pilots an open invitation to a duck blind at the club. When the pilots did go to Long Beach, they'd head for the pike or "nightly muster" at the Breakers Hotel's Skytop Room, whose 360-degree view was also enjoyed by celebrities like Clark Gable, Rita Hayworth, Errol Flynn and Cary Grant.

Senior pilots might head up to Los Angeles or Hollywood to meet up with ladies they had met from Chaplain Erdman's Hope and Crosby Hollywood connections. But ensigns (even with flight pay) couldn't afford to do that very often.

Some pilots needed encouragement to head off base. One Saturday, Hal Silvert left the BOQ to head to a movie on the base. Near the theater, Redbird Burnette, spiffed up in his dress blues with a mirror-like shine on his shoes, fell in beside Silvert and said, "Listen, kid, I want to tell you something very important. When we get out to sea for those long days and nights, you know what you'll remember? You will remember every single night you went to the movies!" Silvert told Winters, "That was my last movie."

Some had interaction with Los Alamitos women. Bomber pilot Lieutenant Bill Emerson remembered "one young lady fondly, but I don't think her father approved very much of ensign naval aviators."

If funds were too short, the pilots hit the main BOQ bar or invited attractive ladies to a VF party at the Officers' Club. On such occasions, the group's intelligence officer, former Chicago stockbroker Jack Wheeler,

A Brief History of Los Alamitos and Rossmoor

pulled out a slot machine with the standard cherries, bells and fruits replaced with different Japanese attack planes. They dubbed the one-armed bandit a "Visual Aid Recognition Machine (VARM)." Winters kept it locked up in his office along with classified matter and whiskey but broke it out for VF parties.

In February 1944, Air Group 19 headed for Hawaii and further training in newer, faster planes. It also broke in some new pilots and continued its "Alamitos tradition" of parties and colorful "off-duty" behavior. Finally, in late June 1944, the group was sent into combat duty, based aboard the *Lexington*, the flagship for Vice Admiral Mark Mitscher's Fast Carrier Task Force, the largest naval fleet ever assembled. The task force also included the carriers *Essex*, *Langley* and *Princeton*.

The Nineteenth, which replaced a very successful group, began racking up its own kills, first over Palau, the Bonins (Iwo Jima, Chi Chi Jima and Ha Ha Jima) and then in a month of raids over the Philippines. They suffered horrible casualties. Redbird Burnette and Joe Kelley were shot down over the Bonins. The former died in his plane, but the latter was captured, beheaded and ordered boiled and eaten by the sadistic Japanese commander there.

In two months of action, the "Fighting 19" saw as much action as many units saw throughout the entire war. But they were just getting started. The next thirty days would be the most successful in the history of American fighter aviation. October 24, and the Battle of Leyte Gulf, was the single most destructive day in modern naval history. Group 19 pilots helped sink three Japanese carriers, two of which had participated in the attack on Pearl Harbor. U.S. forces claimed a total of seventeen Japanese ships, totaling 183,000 tons. American forces lost five ships and 22,456 tons.

During September and October, the task force flew seventeen thousand sorties. But in early November, the Lex was hit by a kamikaze plane that killed eleven air group pilots and injured many more. Finished as a viable air squadron, VF-19 was ordered home for leave, regrouping, refitting and retraining.

Air Group 19 was one of the most decorated Air Groups of World War II. It boasted eleven air aces and earned seventeen Navy Crosses,

The Base

ten Silver Stars, thirty-one Distinguished Flying Crosses and twenty-four Air Medals.

In four months, the fighters recorded 155 air-to-air victories, sank five Japanese navy ships and twenty-five cargo ships and damaged ninety-seven thousand pounds of shipping. Their 155 kills in just over four months ranked them eighth among all fighter squadrons in the number of kills per single deployment. The fighters' proudest achievement, though, was that no bomber or torpecker was ever shot down while being escorted by the fighters of VF-19. But Winters said the fighters were equally proud of the bomber and torpedo pilots, who ran up a score of thirteen enemy planes shot down to zero of their own.

In mid-1943, NAS Los Al's mission was changed from elimination/training to carrier support. The majority of Los Al–trained pilots became replacements in established units, but one group that trained and fought together from beginning to the end was Air Group 19, composed of fighters, dive bombers and torpedo bombers. After training at Los Al from August 1943 to February 1944, the group shipped to the South Pacific and participated in some of the largest naval air battles of World War II. Based aboard the USS *Lexington*, Group 19's pilots recorded 155 air-to-air victories, and sunk thirty ships, including three carriers, one of which the super-carrier Zuikaku had participated in the raid on Pearl Harbor. After a kamikaze attack on "the *Lex*" devastated the unit, Air Group 19 was sent back to the States to regroup. But in its four months of fighting, Air Group 19 was one of the most decorated of World War II. It boasted eleven air aces and earned seventeen Navy Crosses, ten Silver Stars, thirty-one Distinguished Flying Crosses and twenty-four Air Medals.

A Brief History of Los Alamitos and Rossmoor

Back at Los Al, the station continued to churn out battle-qualified pilots—this time intended as replacements for the carrier-based air units creeping closer and closer to Japan. They were assigned to carriers like *San Jacinto, Hancock, Bunker Hill, Enterprise* and many others.

The base's support personnel continued to grow. By late 1944, over eighty WAVES were at the base working as storekeepers, mechanics, bus drivers, radio operators, pharmacist's mates and tower operators.

Down the road, the U.S. Navy saw another need for the wide-open land that still remained south of the base. In early 1944, it bought 3,500 acres around Anaheim Bay and the flat acreage up to Ocean Avenue (now the 405/22 freeway) from the Hellman family and built a new base and wharf for the storing and loading of ammunition for U.S. naval ships and for providing anti-submarine, anti-torpedo nets for the stationary bases at sea. Commissioned late in the same year, it helped the war effort but provided another buffer to isolate the Los Alamitos–Seal Beach area from the rest of Orange County.

And like Los Al and all the other local military bases, it allowed thousands of people to experience for themselves the pleasant weather and lifestyle of California and helped jumpstart the next phase of our story.

9
AFTER THE WAR: THE RACETRACK AND SMALL TOWN, USA

With World War II over, activity at the base was scaled back and some of the town's locals who had served in the military began to return.

Bobby Campbell and brother-in-law Harland Huber resumed civilian life and helped open the new and larger Campbell's Market at the corner of Florista and Los Al Boulevard. Their new store was on the same block as Long's Trailer Park. In 1940, Coy Long moved from Fullerton to Los Alamitos and purchased the Watts Brothers' general store on the east side of Los Al Boulevard near Florista. Long operated the store with his two sons, Vernon and Charles . In the late 1940's, Charles (more often called Chuck), spent time in Europe on military duty.

Some of the returning soldiers decided to form a Los Alamitos chapter of the American Legion, which was formally chartered as Post 716 in January 1947. They held their first meetings in the Community Church building. The post organized hospital visits and sponsored the town's first Boy Scout troop. In November 1949, the members voted to rename the chapter to honor two of the town's soldiers who didn't make it back from the war in the South Pacific: Delphino Marin, who died in 1942, in New Guinea, and Lonnie (Bud) Davis, who died in March 1944 on Bougainville Island. In 1948, a posthumous ceremony was held at the Community Church for Davis. Many articles in the *Press-Telegram* noted that Post 716 was a very active chapter, especially the ladies' auxiliary, often led by Rose Watte and Mrs. Lee Ellis. They held bazaars and dances—sometimes at Laurel School and then, after October 1949, at the newly opened St. Isidore's Parish Hall. When the Korean War broke out and the threat of communism appeared to loom even larger, Mrs. Ellis stepped up to be the block warden for the area's new civilian defense program.

By late 1949, Chuck Long had served his two years in the U.S. Army and returned to Los Alamitos, where he helped his dad build one of the area's first "supermarkets" across the boulevard but closer to Katella. The Longs also installed a trailer park on the rest of their property (where Preveza and the Radio Shack are currently located). For a short period, one of their trailer park residents was the Amazing Kimo, a circus animal trainer who kept some of his baby tigers in cages behind his trailer. Jim Bell Jr. remembers going over to watch Kimo work on his act with the young tigers.

But for Bell and other youngsters in the area, the wooded area around Coyote Creek and the river was still the best playground a kid could have—with lots of trees and shrubs, it was a great place to hide, hunt, play and sometimes picnic.

But that would soon change, as would many other things in Los Alamitos. Death and taxes made sure of that.

Immediately after the war, corporate taxes were running at 77 percent, leaving the owners of the Los Alamitos Sugar Company in a tough position. The factory was no longer producing, and its leased farmland was hardly profitable once taxes were paid. Clark Bonner and the other owners decided to begin selling off the assets of the Sugar Company and the Montana Land Company.

Bonner died in 1947, but his wife and the remaining Clark heirs stayed the course. Among the first items sold was the Los Alamitos sugar factory. In 1926, it shipped its beet processing business to the Holly Company's Santa Ana factory, and by the late 1930s, it had moved most of its beet growing to the Imperial Valley. So in April 1948, new company president Gus Strodthoff oversaw the sales of the factory property around Los Alamitos to a series of Southern California real

After the War

For his second season (in 1952), Vessels was granted fourteen days, but if he donated one race's proceeds to a charity, he was awarded an additional day. Vessels proposed donating proceeds from one race to the Grace Johnson Youth Center still being formed by Los Alamitos residents. But state law wouldn't permit funds to go to an entity named after an individual, so Grace Johnson's name was dropped, and the organization was renamed the Los Alamitos Youth Center. Vessels not only gave them funds from the races, but he also sent over crews to finish construction of their building. This photo was taken from the west. Note how the grandstand faces the afternoon sun. In 1954, Vessels built a new track and luxurious grandstand (facing away from the sun) north of the Southern Pacific tracks.

estate investors. The sugar equipment and other company assets were sold to the Holly Sugar Company.

In 1949 the Montana Ranch, ten square miles of land northwest of Los Alamitos, was sold for $8.8 million to three builders—Ben Weingart, Mark Taper and Louis Boyar—who built the "instant city" of Lakewood.

But Bonner did dispose of at least one parcel before he died. In mid-April 1946, he sold the company's three-hundred-acre East Ranch, located on Katella east of Bloomfield and south of the tracks, to horseman Frank Vessels.

Vessels came to California from Kentucky in 1920 after the Signal Hill and Huntington Beach oil booms. He found success building boilers for oil-drilling platforms. During World War II, his company, OFCCO (Oil Fields Construction Company), cornered the market for building boilers on the many new military posts being constructed on the Pacific Coast.

A Brief History of Los Alamitos and Rossmoor

While he lived and worked in Long Beach, he owned a polled Hereford cattle ranch in Corona until one of his engineers got him interested in quarter horses. After a deal for a large parcel in East Long Beach around Palo Verde and Los Coyotes Diagonal fell through, Vessels bought the three-hundred-acre spread just east of Los Alamitos in April 1946 to house his growing stable of quarter horses. He occasionally kept some polled Hereford at his new ranch for fattening, and in mid-1948, he had to post a warning in the *Enterprise* to the new neighbors around him: his cattle could be mean—leave them alone. Mainly, he raised quarter horses at the new ranch, and in 1947, he began holding "betless" Sunday races, which became quite popular; one in July 1948 drew an estimated 2,500 spectators. Vessels, who by now had become president of the Pacific Coast Quarter Horse Association, tried to get state approval for parimutuel betting but was constantly thwarted by the Southern California Thoroughbred Track owners and trainers. In late October 1951, through a lot of behind-the-scenes political wrangling (and some

In 1946, Frank Vessels bought over three hundred acres of the Montana Land Company's East Ranch to train his quarter horses. On August 3, 1947, Vessels began hosting Sunday "betless" match races on a half-mile oval training track and was soon drawing as many as 2,500 attendees. In 1951, over heavy opposition from Southern California thoroughbred interests, Vessels was licensed to host an eleven-day meet with parimutuel betting. Despite heavy rain for ten of the eleven days, the meet averaged over 3,000 attendees per day, and from that start Los Alamitos would grow to become the center of American Quarter Horse Racing on the Pacific Coast.

alleged payoffs to California legislators), state racing officials finally granted Vessels permission to hold an eleven-day parimutuel meeting in early December, just five weeks away.

That first parimutuel meeting at Los Alamitos was pelted by constant rain, but Vessels pulled it off and was granted fourteen days of racing the following year. Vessels put another $100,000 of improvements into his facility. That 1952 meeting saw business double over the previous meet, and quarter horse racing in California had found a home. He also extended his meet by two days because racetracks were allowed to be open an additional day if a race on that day aided a charity. This began a long association with the Los Alamitos Youth Center.

A little to the west, death and taxes were again bringing more change to the area.

In 1947, Susannah Bixby Bryant died. Facing major tax issues, Bryant's children began selling off her property. The estate arranged with Long Beach developer Lloyd Whaley to develop the Bryant land in Los Angeles County into the new community of Los Altos. A partnership that included the Irvine Company bought Bryant's land near Los Alamitos.

In 1948, also facing tax issues, the Bixby Land Company started selling its available land just south of the Long Beach Airport.

Although a little slower, change inevitably came to the Fred Bixby ranch. Many of the same families—the Napoles, the Wattes, Sisneros—still worked the Bixbys' Alamitos land. Florence still made sure every child had food and schooling. The families still came for Christmas celebrations at the main house, and in 1949, 1,100 guests—family members, friends, former tenants—showed up for Fred and Florence's fiftieth wedding anniversary.

A year before, to help secure a new state college in Long Beach (over a competing offer from Downey), city leaders asked Fred Bixby to donate some of his good mesa land. He finally did so and this began the final dismantling of the Fred Bixby Ranch.

Fred passed away in May 1952, and control of the Bixby Ranch Company shifted to his very able son-in-law, Preston Hotchkis Sr. Hotchkis was a successful insurance businessman, a frequent president of the Southern California Chamber of Commerce and very involved in the Metropolitan Water District's plan to secure Colorado River water.

He was influential in Republican Party affairs, and in later years, he would become a trusted advisor to Ronald Reagan, when the latter was governor and later president. Hotchkis had married Fred Bixby's oldest daughter, Katharine, and they lived in San Marino.

In the 1930s, Fred had set up a trust, carving out 140 acres around the old Bixby adobe house on the hill to preserve it for future generations, but the next generation faced some realities the previous one hadn't. As Fred's daughter Katharine said, "Condemnations gobbled up acres of land, freeways squeezed against the boundaries. Taxes skyrocketed. And—so sad—he [Fred Bixby] forgot one thing—his children grew up, they got married, they moved away and had their own children and lives full of their own obligations, responsibilities and interests."

"Scores of new people" were moving into the Los Alamitos area. The war had given a large number of men a taste of the pleasant Southern California weather, and many returned to find well-paying jobs in the region's booming economy at companies like Douglas Aircraft. Those former servicemen took advantage of the GI Bill, which let them buy a new home with no money down.

In late 1947, a new tract of homes began, whose 321 units "would double Los Alamitos' population." The first phase of the Alamos Ranchos (81 units with prices beginning at $7,500) started just outside the gates of the base, covering Lexington and the three blocks to the east. They quickly sold out, and in March 1948, plans were announced for 104 more—although the builders said the county must step in and provide a sewer system. Without it, development in West Orange County "is a dead issue."

In April, local newspapers reported that Mr. and Mrs. Charles Hancock of Long Beach had the "honor of being the first family to move into the new Alamos Rancho subdivision and several others are now following suit." Enough came that in May the school district had to buy a new bus to handle the increase in traffic.

A severe cold snap in late 1948 motivated the new homeowners—who included many veterans—to form an association to complain in force about the faulty heating systems and poor drainage. The subcontractors adjusted the heaters, and the county built some curbs, but the developers reportedly lost enough money and gained a bad enough reputation that

After the War

they felt a new name was necessary. A second phase, two years later, was called Plainview Homes. A third, in 1955, was called Los Alamitos Park. They all looked alike, and over time, all three phases together, a total of 321 homes, became known as Carrier Row since its streets—Lexington, Essex, Ranger, Saratoga, et al—were named for the flattops affiliated with the Los Al naval air units.

In October 1944, a number of men in the town officially organized the Los Alamitos Volunteer Fire Department. They raised enough money to purchase a 1929 Model A truck for $345 and put a water pump on the back of it. In March 1945, they purchased a lot on the boulevard and paid out $5 to rent the Laurel School auditorium for a dance, where they raised money to buy more fire equipment.

On Saturday,, May 8, 1948, the town dedicated the new adobe block firehouse. Two hundred people attended an afternoon open house, and "a large crowd attended the dance in the evening," where music was provided by the Los Alamitos Naval Air Band and Orchestra. Proceeds from the event, sponsored by the department's Women's Auxiliary, "went towards new fire-fighting equipment." It would be the first of many dances at the town's new de facto social hall. "Because it was a county building, you couldn't have drinks inside," remembered Marilynn Poe. "But all the dads would have their cars lined up behind the building with their trunks up, each acting as a bar."

Laurel School was still used for adult dances at times. The new Los Alamitos Homeowners Association held one there in 1948 with a band from the U.S. Navy base providing music.

The town's former dance hall, the sugar factory clubhouse, which hosted social dances and gatherings for many years, was now a sanitarium (what would now be called an assisted living facility).

Los Alamitos was growing. By 1947, Long's and Campbell's were not the only markets vying for the community's grocery business. So was DeWitt's Market (eventually sold to the Rees Bros.). A few years later, if you wanted a good cut of meat, you could also go to Cecil's Meats (where Imperial Jewelers is now).

Louise Slette moved her Marie's Café ("Best food in town," said Jim Bell Jr.) business north of Katella. Dominie DeBruyn moved from

Westminster and ran a café called the Wander Inn. In the mid-1940s, he purchased the old Felts' Store Building at the corner of Reagan and Florista and moved it to the west side of the boulevard, south of Catalina, and renamed it DeBruyn's Café. (It would later become the Los Alamitos Inn.) In 1950, Louisa Aguilar opened an eatery as well, but sometime before that, the Wander Inn underwent a name change to the Airport Café (operated by Clarence Humphrey). It survived a fire and reopened, then later survived another change to a bar called the Boondocks, an establishment which now has an almost mythical yet mysterious status among locals, who ask, "Who actually goes in there?" and "Why does it always seem busy when I pass by it while driving my kids to school in the morning?"

Other new businesses were also opening. Returning vet Dick Fulford and his wife opened a beverage store. Bud Cook opened a toy and hobby shop. The City Garden Acres Tract continued to grow. In 1947, a transplant from West Tennessee, Jim Bell, took a job as a civilian electrician at the base and bought a home on Farquhar, which was still a dirt road. When the four o'clock bell rang, the traffic on Farquhar would kick up so much dirt that it was almost impossible to do laundry and let it dry on the outside clotheslines. He approached chamber of commerce secretary Grace Johnson about getting Farquhar paved. Johnson was a former vaudeville stage performer who had been involved with the Los Al chamber "since long before World War II." In 1940, her husband, John, operated a café, and she was an attendant at the public library, but during the war, with so many men off in the military, Grace had basically acted as a "one-woman chamber." Johnson was involved with many other activities, including the nineteen-member volunteer fire department, where she was awarded Badge 14, being the only woman ever so honored. When Bell contacted her in mid-1947, she informed him that the chamber was trying to reactivate itself. Roy Wright had just been selected president, and they were looking for new members. Bell signed on.

In 1948, the twenty-one local businessmen had also started a Business Association. Their first meeting was a breakfast hosted by sanitarium owner A.A. Guilliaum. Grocer Cleo DeWitt was elected president of the new group, August Labourdette his vice-president and Johnson, secretary-treasurer. Frank Watte, Jack Baird and Louis Aguilar were the publicity committee. The group liked meeting for breakfast but noted there was no café open at those hours that could serve that large a group. The problem was resolved when DeBruyn's Café said it would open for the meetings, which the group decided would be twice a month. Among the Business Association's first actions were to sponsor a men's softball team and get a directory and business map of the town. A couple months later, apparently having caught up with their backlog of pressing business, the group decided to meet only once a month—but not before voting to sponsor a three-day October community carnival, which turned out to be a big success, despite the heat. Seven rides, fourteen booths, steaks barbecued to order and an auction whose donated items included a calf, a pig and a one-hundred-pound sack of lima beans—how could it not be fun? The climax of the event was a drawing for a free television set.

Fresh off their big success, the businessmen soon agreed to become a sub-group of the chamber of commerce.

In the following June 1949, the chamber's longtime secretary, Grace Johnson, died. During the war, with so many gone, she had been instrumental in keeping the chamber together, and afterward she had been the secretary and treasurer of that group, the Businessman's Association and the Volunteer Firemen's Auxiliary. The night before her death she was collecting tickets at the inaugural dance of the Alamos Ranch Homeowners Association.

To honor her, the chamber organized a meeting of seven town organizations who all agreed to work together to construct the Grace Johnson Youth Center. The new building, to be located on land donated by William C. Poe, on Katella Avenue just across from Laurel School, would be used for adult meetings, as well as for youth activities. Soon, enough money was raised to pour a foundation and a slab floor for the new center. Restrooms were also partially completed, and then the funds ran out. But that didn't stop the kids or the town from using just the slab for dances, meetings and festivals.

Johnson was so popular in town with the town's youth and did so many duties that many old-timers remain convinced that she was the town's

A Brief History of Los Alamitos and Rossmoor

The Los Alamitos Volunteer Fire Department was officially organized in 1944, and funds were raised to purchase the Model A truck shown above and a pump to put in the back. Using money raised at a town dance at Laurel School, the town also purchased a lot to store the new fire truck. In May 1948, the county dedicated the new adobe brick firehouse. To fund the purchase of new equipment like resuscitators, the ladies' auxiliary would hold dances at the new station. Because it was a county building, you couldn't have drinks inside, but the men would have their cars lined up behind the building with their trunks up, each acting as a bar.

"Santa Claus," a woman who every holiday season would don the Santa costume and make personal visits to the houses of the town's children. But in January 1949, Johnson herself, with the chamber, presented an award to Alice Tischler for her service as the "spirit of Christmas" and for selfless service in traveling "so many hundreds of miles during the Yule season in making appearances."

The loss of Johnson was large but not irreplaceable, as Lura Labourdette, the daughter of City Garden Acres promoter Rush Green

After the War

and now the wife of August Labourdette (owner of A.J. Supply), stepped in and became the chamber's secretary-manager and filled Johnson's former roles very ably.

She was aided in her work by Jim Bell. After joining the chamber in 1947, he immersed himself in library books that showed the political process to get a street paved. By 1951, he had become president of the chamber and, with secretary-manager Lura Labourdette (the daughter of Rush Green), helped revitalize that organization into an effective, quasi-local government. Bell would be president seven times over the next ten years, but he shared the gavel with attorney William C. Poe Jr., Chuck Long and others. Working with Orange County supervisor Willis Warner, the chamber got Farquhar paved and led the way to get streetlights (1951), a water district and a sewer system (1952).

Labourdette was very resourceful, and played a major role in getting the town's first traffic light. When county workers installed a trip to measure traffic at the intersection, Labourdette got on the phone and told everyone in town to repeatedly drive over the trip and then over it again to make sure the count was large enough to get that traffic light.

Jack Baird was a real estate agent and insurance man who moved back from Long Beach in the late 1940s, convinced that Los Alamitos had a great future. In 1951, he had moved into a brand-new combination home office at the southeast corner of Los Alamitos Boulevard and Howard Street. It was one of the first designs by the soon-to-be world-famous architect Edward Killingsworth, who would go on to design much of Long Beach State and many large hotels like the Kahala Hilton in Hawaii. Baird's house/office was featured in newspapers and magazines and won many awards for its interpretation of post-and-beam design and floor-to-ceiling windows. Baird's daughter (and Killingsworth's wife) Laura made a reputation for herself as one of the leading performers in musical theater in Long Beach and throughout Southern California over the next thirty years. But Jim Bell Jr. most remembers that Baird's home/office had a floor-to-ceiling window, and he was also one of the first persons in the area to have a television: "Every afternoon after school, kids would huddle around his front window, and Mr. Baird would roll the TV over so we could watch the cartoon shows."

A Brief History of Los Alamitos and Rossmoor

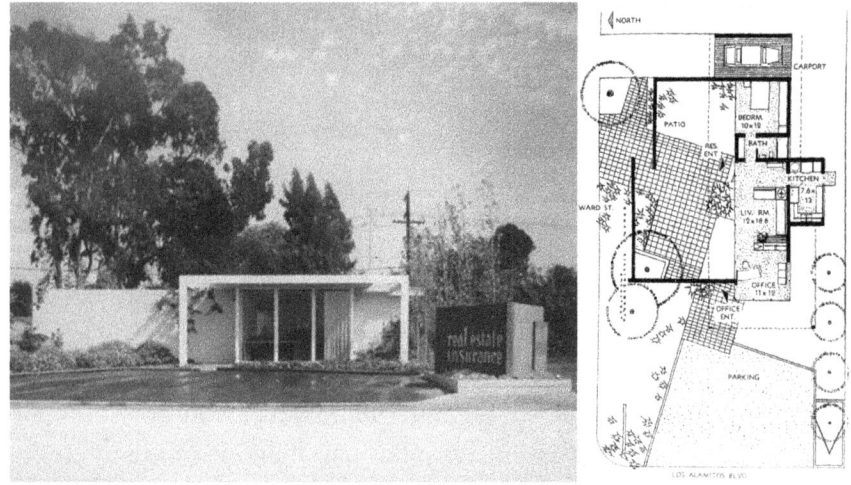

In 1951, realtor/insurance man Jack Baird moved into a combination home/office at the southwest corner of Los Alamitos Boulevard and Green Street. It was one of the first designs by soon-to-be-world-famous architect Edward Killingsworth, who would go on to design much of Long Beach State and many large hotels like the Kahala Hilton in Hawaii. Baird's house/office was featured in newspapers and magazines and won many architectural awards for its interpretation of post-and-beam design and floor-to-ceiling windows. But Jim Bell Jr. most remembers that Baird was also one of the first persons in the area to have a television: "Every afternoon after school, kids would huddle around his big front window, and Mr. Baird would roll the TV over so we could watch the cartoon shows." The building is now an orthodontist's office.

In 1950, the town had another new tract of homes. Developer Max Nessel, who had built some of the homes south of the Long Beach airport, bought some more land from the Bixby Land Company, this parcel across Los Alamitos Boulevard from the old factory. With architect Robert Levy, Nessel built a ninety-two-home tract called Los Alamitos Terrace, with most of the homes north of Catalina (behind the current Shenandoah at the Arbor).

A short time after all the remaining sugar factory equipment was auctioned off, automobile trailer pioneer Curtis Wright (he is credited with resurrecting the Airstream brand of auto trailers immediately after the war) announced a venture in January 1949 to build "light motor cars" at the old sugar factory plant. (This Curtis Wright had no connection to the large Curtiss-Wright aircraft manufacturer, but confusion wasn't discouraged.) Just two years previously, he had introduced a flying car—a three-wheel vehicle with folding rotor blades that he called a fly-mobile. It didn't catch on. His new prototype car was reportedly capable of seventy-five miles per hour and forty miles to the gallon, and its "two curved parts"—its hood and a hood-and-front-fender combination—were made of colored plastic and the doors of plywood to keep it lightweight. Like its fly-mobile predecessor, the boxy shapeless auto may have been ahead of—or far behind—its time, but it didn't catch on either. Within a few months, Wright sold his trailer operation, and little was heard from him again.

After the war, the navy base was scaled down and returned to reserve station status. On June 26, 1948, it marked the two-year anniversary of that designation with one of "the biggest dances ever held in Southern California." Hangar 2 was cleared out to provide forty thousand square feet of dancing to the music of big band legend Jimmy Dorsey. Twelve speakers made sure that all the military dignitaries and civilians from town could hear every note and sax solo from Dorsey's unit. The event was also a carnival, with prizes including trips to Mexico (courtesy of Pan-Am Airways) and radio-phonograph combinations, not to mention all-electric irons. All proceeds benefited Navy Relief.

But with the start of the Korean War in 1950, serious activity quickly ramped up again. Veteran pilots were recalled en masse, including Baseball Hall of Famer Jerry Coleman. In November 1950, an entire reserve unit from San Diego, Fighter Squadron VF-783, volunteered to re-up—and it was assigned for new training at Los Alamitos, where the men got in their hours on the new jets that were being rolled out. Some of the Los Al trained units served in Korea, flying Corsairs from carriers like the *Bonhomme Richard* "during the UN's darkest days." Over the next few years, Los Al was the U.S. Navy's busiest reserve air base. Jets were introduced and then helicopters.

But even after the Korean conflict ended, NAS Los Alamitos remained busy. In late 1955 and 1956, future astronaut Neil Armstrong, who would be the first man to walk on the moon, flew weekend hours with a Los Al reserve unit and then went up to Muroc (now Edwards) Air Force Base, where he worked weekdays as a test pilot.

A Brief History of Los Alamitos and Rossmoor

After drastically scaling down at the end of World War II, NAS Los Al had to gear up quickly for the Korean War and it became the nation's busiest naval reserve air station and remained so throughout the 1950s, training pilots in jet airplanes. Among the pilots who flew at Los Al were two future astronauts, Neil Armstrong, who would become the first man to walk on the moon in 1969, and Marine Major John Glenn Jr. (above right) who broke the record for a transcontinental flight in 1957 on a day that began at NAS Los Alamitos.

On July 16, 1957, another future astronaut, U.S. Marine pilot John Glenn, flew an F8U-1 Crusader from Los Alamitos to New York in three hours, twenty-three minutes and 8.4 seconds, setting a new transcontinental speed. The flight was covered with a big spread in *Life* magazine and the newsreels.

The base even conducted early tests for one-man helicopters, including the experimental Grillo model, which was featured in newsreels. Hugh Winters, the former commander of Air Group 19, was reassigned and helped organize the Blue Angels, a group that would appear at many of the air shows held at Los Alamitos, sometimes in conjunction with the National Model Airplane Show.

Of course, with more personnel, there were more sports. Future Basketball Hall of Famer George Yardley (Newport Beach, Stanford and the Detroit Pistons) led the base basketball team to two straight national AAU championship tournaments. The "Air Raiders" got big headlines and played before crowds at Long Beach City College and the Convention Center; they were ducked by college teams like USC and UCLA. The

After the War

In the early 1950s, Los Alamitos was the site of training on some of the earliest one-man helicopters (left). Because Los Alamitos was the closest military base to Hollywood, it got many celebrity visitors. Bob Hope frequently did his weekly live radio show from the base, although sometimes renaming the site so it didn't seem he was playing favorites. In 1953, he not only came to the base solo to help recruiting (shown above), but he also did a radio show with Rosemary Clooney.

Los Al team played only six players, but they included former USC standout Dick Eby and Long Island University (via Los Angeles City College) players Hal Uplinger and Al Rogers. But "Jumping George" Yardley was the man. During their regular 1953 season, the Naval Flyers suffered only one loss and became the first service team to reach the AAU championship game in forty-six years, taking on the Peoria Diesel Cats, a squad sponsored by the Caterpillar Tractor Company and the most dominant AAU basketball team in the early 1950s. The Cats won five national titles in a time when AAU ball was considered by many to be equal in quality to the NBA, and their starting five had all been named to the United States team for the 1952 Helsinki Olympics.

In the 1953 AAU championship match, Yardley scored twenty-nine points and received a standing ovation from the appreciative crowd in Denver, but the Los Al five fell 73–62. Yardley was also one of the stars on a very good base volleyball squad, which won the all-service championship.

The base also fielded bowling teams and would win national titles in water polo (led by Wally Wolf, a member of the 1948 Olympic team) and women's ping-pong. It was also home to Olympic medal-winning sprinters like hurdler Art Bernard.

A Brief History of Los Alamitos and Rossmoor

As if it wasn't busy enough, in 1957, guards at the base even reported a UFO sighting.

The base was busier than ever, but by now many jobs at NAS Los Alamitos had been taken over by civilians.

By 1951, the Fall Festival and Carnival featured a parade with the Long Beach Mounted Police and the Long Beach Lancerettes and a number of marching units. Frank Vessels and dairyman Victor Vandermaele were the parade chairmen. The youth center still had no walls or roof, so merchants and organizations had booths around the outside edge. High schooler Kay Stockton was crowned Festival Queen at a ceremony on the Youth Center slab.

The town wanted to build walls on the slab, but funds were short—until Vessels stepped in. State law allowed him to add a day of racing if one of the races benefitted a charity, but not one named after a person. In February 1952, Youth Center president Roy Wright dedicated the plaque commemorating Grace Johnson at the newly renamed Los Alamitos Youth Center, and very soon after, using money from the charity horse race and the donated labor from Frank Vessels's crews, the walls and ceiling of the new center finally went up, and it was soon completed.

In 1954, the Youth Center also began sponsoring a boys' baseball team, which participated in the Long Beach Police Athletic League and Rec Leagues. Young Bill Poe III and Nick Haagsma coached one of these teams. "We were too old to play just as players. But if we coached, they let us play," Poe remembers. A number of adult men played fast-pitch softball on a team sponsored by the Anaheim Optimists. Managed by Bennie Marin (unlike his brother Delfino, he fortunately survived World War II duty, although in the Navy), the team won the Anaheim League five years in a row. Other locals on the team were Bob Austin, Sanchez, Walt DeBruyn and Johnny Haagsma. By now, organized sports were big in Los Alamitos. Beginning in 1948, Laurel School sponsored both a football and basketball team. For the latter, school superintendent Jack L. Weaver proudly announced that the school had paved two basketball courts and would compete against Cypress, Savanna, Stanton, Magnolia, Westminster and Ocean View schools.

Most of the town's events were getting newspaper coverage—at first in the *LA Times*, *Santa Ana Register*, *Anaheim Bulletin* and the two Long

After the War

Beach papers—the *Press-Telegram* and the *Independent*. Then, in March 1948, the West Orange County Newspaper Group (which had published the *Los Alamitos Press* in the late 1920s but by now had dwindled from five local papers to one, the Buena Park *News)* decided to give West County its own paper.

Soon after the war, the company was bought by Paul Kroesen, a recent immigrant from Iowa, where his father had edited newspapers for years. Paul Kroesen edited the Buena Park paper and, in March 1948, assigned his sister, Beth, to be editor of a new version of the *Cypress Enterprise*. The first year and a half featured regular coverage of Los Alamitos, but the paper was promoted as a Cypress paper, and by mid-1949, Los Alamitos coverage had dwindled to almost nothing. This might have played a part in the debut of a new paper in Los Alamitos: the *Nickelodeon*. Started in early 1950 by Ray Watson, the *Nickelodeon* was a weekly eight-page tabloid newspaper that seemingly covered every Los Alamitos event and issue. Shooting the Breeze with Pappy Reeves, a weekly column, kept the town informed of base activities. In April 1950, the paper marked Campbell's Market's fifteenth anniversary and reminded residents to protest the latest (San Diego) freeway plan, which left Los Alamitos and Stanton "high and dry." Where the *Enterprise* had very few Los Alamitos advertisers, the *Nickelodeon* had many: the Monte Vista Cleaners, Palm Tree Café (with Eastside beer on tap), Ruth's Malt Shop ("across from the high school, with the best hamburgers in town"), Morrel Photography and Denny's Toys.

Sometime after 1952, the *Nickelodeon* disappeared, and by January 1954 the *Enterprise* had changed its title to the *Los Alamitos–Cypress Enterprise*, now edited by Dale Kroesen. Dale had served a previous stint as editor of the paper, signing on in mid-1949 after getting discharged from a three-year U.S. Air Force hitch, including two years in India. But in January 1952, he left to work as publicist for a local company. Either he had too much printer's blood in his veins or the other job didn't pay, because by New Years 1954, Dale Kroesen had brought his dry wit back to the editor's position at the expanded *Enterprise*.

The Kroesens were active in the community. In 1952, Paul was president of the Buena Park Chamber of Commerce, while Dale headed the Cypress chamber. Over the next few years, Dale would become equally active in the Los Alamitos chamber as well. He also bought the *Enterprise* from his brother and moved its offices to Los Alamitos, near Marie's Café. By the mid-1950s, the *Enterprise* had the Los Alamitos local news market to itself.

Los Alamitos soon had a third church. In 1948, Jim Bell and some others helped start and build the First Baptist Church in the City Garden Acres tract, which in 1953 had twenty new homes under construction, as realtor Jack Baird told the *Press-Telegram*, adding that twenty-four new homes were ready for occupancy in the Old Town West area.

Floods still came—in some ways worse than before. In 1952, the concrete channels upstream contained most of the rain water until it reached where the concrete ended and spilled over the nearby dirt levees and across Los Alamitos and the surrounding dairies. The floods of January 1952 were among the area's worst. "The cow poop was floating

In the late 1940s, Los Alamitos got its third church when the Baptists built a structure at Bloomfield and Howard. Future mayor Jim Bell promoted the church's upcoming Easter Service by driving a replica of the church around the community.

After the War

all over," laughed Marilynn Poe. School was cancelled, and the Navy medical units were called in to duty to provide inoculations—on the base and at the volunteer fire department.

After the floods of January 1952 "inundated the area," money was appropriated to channel the San Gabriel River and Coyote Creek, from Del Amo to just before Seventh Street, where it basically reached sea level and salt water. The work involved widening both channel beds and building higher concrete levees for maximum protection. This would make available for development much farmland around Los Alamitos that was previously undesirable for housing because it was frequently flooded.

The dairy farmers in northwest Orange County began to get worried. Most had already been pushed out once by new subdivisions—from

In early 1952, heavy rainfall once again resulted in the flooding of Coyote Creek and the San Gabriel River over most areas of Los Alamitos, inundating many septic tanks and causing manure from the dairy farms to foul the floodwaters. The base medical personnel provided rescue operations and tetanus shots at the Los Al Fire station.

A Brief History of Los Alamitos and Rossmoor

Torrance and Gardena, Lynwood, Bellflower, Paramount and Norwalk. New homeowners in those areas didn't like the smells of dairy cows.

In the 1940s, many farmers moved into a dairy belt running from present Cerritos down to north Los Alamitos. By the early 1950s, there were about thirty dairy farms in the area, along with a few chicken ranches and some row farmers. But now the new tracts were closing in again, spreading south from Lakewood and east from Long Beach. Spurred by the opening of Disneyland in 1955, Orange County, especially Anaheim, Buena Park and Garden Grove, were growing west through annexations.

To ward off the annexations, the dairymen started forming cities; Dairyland (La Palma) was first in 1955, followed by Dairy Valley (Cerritos). Soon after, the farmers in the Cypress area joined that area's chamber of commerce en masse, turning what had previously been a pro-business and pro-growth group into an anti-growth, anti-annexation organization.

The leaders of Los Alamitos were also worried about annexation, and the chamber organized three attempts at incorporation. The first two were in coordination with other communities and would have taken in a large area of West Orange County. The third, organized in September and October 1955, was smaller and involved only the area around Los Alamitos. The incorporators wanted to include the racetrack within their boundaries and met with Frank Vessels. At this time, he had just expanded his track operation and, in 1954, had built a new, much larger grandstand, which apparently left him strapped for cash. Early Los Alamitos mayors Jim Bell and Chuck Long said Vessels asked the Los Al leaders to forward-fund water and sewer hookups to the track. The Los Al leaders felt they couldn't ethically forward fund this or any investment. The town's early leaders had a very strong "pay as you go" ethic.

At the same time, Cypress/Dairy City leaders were organizing their own incorporation attempt, and they reportedly agreed to Vessels's request, offering him a couple other incentives as well—one being that they wouldn't assess a turnstile tax for some years. Los Al leaders apparently wouldn't agree to this either – you can't offer tax breaks to one and not others. Vessels ended up signing both incorporation petitions but delayed meeting with the Los Alamitos incorporators long enough on October 17, 1955, to make sure their application was submitted to the county clerk one hour and two minutes after the Cypress petition, thus giving Cypress the legal advantage. Los Alamitos filed a protest, but after six weeks, the county ruled for the Cypress incorporators. Their voters would first have the chance to vote on incorporation with the racetrack (and the Texaco Tank farm, as well) within the Cypress boundaries.

Local old-timers assert that Vessels was still peeved at the Los Alamitos leaders for opposing the sale of some seventy-seven acres of his land in May 1955 (between Bloomfield and Lexington) for "a mortuary and Roman Catholic cemetery." The May 27, 1955 *Press-Telegram* does note that the Los Alamitos Chamber of Commerce "registered strong opposition to the projects." Three months later, the August 26, 1955 *Enterprise* reported that Vessels sold sixty-five of those acres to the Guy F. Atkinson Construction Company, a large heavy-construction company that had built freeways and many port-area projects (including part of the Roosevelt and Los Al Navy bases ten years prior) in Los Angeles and Long Beach.

The same sixty-five acres recently made news when it was up for sale for use as a cemetery. Several residents and organizations complained bitterly, and after a heated hearing before the county planning commission, which approved the application, the board of supervisors turned it down.

Since Vessels still sold the property bounded by the school, Lexington, Katella and the SP tracks at a nice price, just how peeved he was with Los Alamitos is still unclear. But longtime Vessels friends (and fellow horsemen), like Marv Haney, say the water issues were more important to him.

In any case, Los Alamitos not only ended up without the racetrack and Tank Farm tax revenues, but also its residents would now have to wait a few years before the next incorporation attempt.

10
ROSS CORTESE AND ROSSMOOR

With the success of Lakewood and the floods of 1952, there was now enough incentive to complete the concrete channelization of the San Gabriel River and Coyote Creek down to the ocean. That combined with another sure act of nature—death—now made all the lands around Los Alamitos available for large-scale development.

The lands on the Long Beach side were worked first. With the proposed Sepulveda (now San Diego) and San Gabriel River freeways cutting out huge swathes of their property and facing huge increases in property taxes, the Fred Bixby heirs made even more land available to continue development.

The heirs of Jotham and Lewellyn Bixby and the Bixby Land Company were also facing increasing tax obligations. The company's new leader, Llewellyn Bixby Jr., solved many of those problems by selling off land in the East Long Beach and West Orange County area (keeping corner lots that could be used for gas stations and small stores). They also traded to Long Beach the low-lying land that would become El Dorado Park (which was originally named Los Alamitos Park). This gained a tax advantage that was utilized to buy land in the Imperial Valley and helped to put the company back on a sound financial basis.

At the time, all of these new developments were still beyond the Long Beach city limits. Because Lakewood was getting national attention, the

Ross Cortese and Rossmoor

Aldus Company called its new development (between Bellflower and Studebaker) Lakewood Plaza. And the Lakewood Rancho Estates were built by a new player on the scene: Ross W. Cortese.

Cortese was a builder best known for his creation of Rossmoor and then the Leisure World empire, and he was ultimately honored as one of the twenty-five most influential figures in the American housing industry—on a list that included Presidents Franklin D. Roosevelt and Woodrow Wilson.

Friends and foes used many terms to describe Cortese—tenacious, visionary, a perfectionist. He was disparaged by some as an egotist and by others as quiet and generous. Still others noted his temper and willingness to butt heads if that's what it took to get things done right.

His official biography notes that he was born in 1916 in East Palestine, Ohio. His Italian immigrant parents moved to California when he was

Builder Ross Cortese personified the American dream. Born to poor immigrant parents, he became one of the largest builder-developers in the nation and set the standard for building and marketing suburban subdivisions. After testing the waters on a smaller scale with the Lakewood Rancho Estates (Spring and Studebaker) and Frematic Homes near Disneyland, Cortese went for the gold with Rossmoor—at the time the largest single development ever built in Orange County and still one of the biggest ever as a single tract. Cortese perfected many of the marketing effects still used today—fully decorated model homes and regular full-page ads in the Sunday newspaper.

young. Some reports say he lived in both Long Beach and Glendale. At the end of his sophomore year, he dropped out of Hoover High School in Glendale to help his father sell produce from a pushcart.

His daughter Heidi recites the tale a little differently: "The family story is he was born on the ship while his parents were emigrating from Italy. Once they got to Ohio, they recorded the paperwork to show my dad was born here, to make sure he was a citizen."

Heidi also says he dropped out of school in the seventh grade and took a job in Long Beach to help his family: "His sisters told me he used to buy them treats and would let them have the bed while he slept on concrete in the garage."

While still in his twenties, he began to restore and resell homes in the Compton and Culver City areas. About this time, he met Alona Goetten, an actress-dancer at MGM who was also studying real estate development at night.

Though Alona was ten years his senior, the pair was soon married. During the war, Alona owned and operated a florist shop in Los Feliz, and Ross worked as a draftsman on a number of government construction jobs. At about this same time, the pair started to travel in more affluent social circles.

Alona's older sister, Gisela, had been a movie star. As "June Marlowe," Gisela had starred in silent films for Universal and Warner Brothers, and after the advent of talkies, she appeared in the Our Gang comedies as the children's teacher, Miss Crabtree. Other family members found work as assistant directors, prop men, set designers and performers. Because of anti-German sentiment during and after World War I, all the Goettens had started using Marlowe as their last name.

In 1933 Gisela/June married businessman husband, Rodney Sprigg who had a large moving and storage business in Hollywood. Heidi Cortese says he was also involved with many boxers, including Jack Dempsey and Gene Tunney. The Spriggs were members of Lakeside Golf Club in Toluca Lake, where over the years Rodney golfed and played cards with friends like Bing Crosby, Bob Hope and John Wayne and June was also a fixture at the club.

Near the end of World War II Alona had obtained her real estate license, and it was under her company name, Alona-Rey homes, that

Ross Cortese and Rossmoor

she and Ross first began remodeling homes in the Los Angeles area and then graduated to building modest single-family homes. They built a small tract in Culver City and another in Downey (under the name Cimcort Corporation) and yet another tract just west of Santa Ana College (English Grove, 1951) under the name Alona Marlowe Cortese Company. Ross Cortese formed the Rossmoor Corporation in 1951, using his first name and the Scottish term most frequently used for an uncultivated area. Another partner in this last company was general contractor Murray Ward, who would handle the building of most of Cortese's projects over the next twenty years.

Whether coincidence or by design, Cortese partnered with a Lakeside Golf Club member, California governor Goodwin Knight, and his Beverly Hills law partner, Alfred Gittelson, to form a new development company. With Lakewood developments being all the rage, the three bought a quarter section of land at the northeast corner of Studebaker and Spring and east of the Lakewood Plaza subdivision. They called their land the Lakewood Rancho Estates. (This land was also adjacent to the future El Dorado Park.)

Like most of the postwar tracts in the Lakewood and East Long Beach area, the homes were originally to be two-bedroom, one-bath or three-bedroom, one-bath homes, ranging in size from 880 to 1,250 square feet on a minimum 5,000-square-foot lot.

But a few weeks into the development, Cortese saw a demonstration by home designers Cliff May and his partner, Chris Choate, of their new prefabricated ranch home design. Impressed, Cortese immediately switched over to the new design.

May was already well known as the acknowledged developer of the original ranch home, many in posh areas of Brentwood and Pacific Palisades. His homes were featured in two books published by *Sunset* magazine. When the custom home market slowed, May and Choate eyed the exploding tract home market and the opportunities from GI loans and modern economics of post-and-beam construction.

The standard home of the time was rectangular, built on raised foundations, with traditional ceilings and attics and oriented toward the street. May's ranch homes were built on L-shaped concrete slabs and

A Brief History of Los Alamitos and Rossmoor

With the Lakewood Rancho Estates, Cortese associated with top-tier architects like Cliff May and Chris Choate (shown at left with a standing Cortese). The ranchos started as conventional raised-foundation homes. But after Cortese saw a demonstration by May and Choate of their new prefabricated ranch home, he became a believer. He stopped production and immediately switched over to the new design. The homes were featured in many magazines, including *Popular Science*.

focused on the backyard. Ceilings in non-bedrooms were often vaulted, and plumbing was encased in the slab floors whose low profile provided a visual continuity from outside to inside and outside again. The continuity was further accentuated by floor-to-ceiling windows, which often made the backyard patio and barbecue an extension of the kitchen or family room. The homes cost $7,500 to build and sold for $11,000.

Cortese sold all seven hundred of the rancho homes in just over two years and caught the notice of architectural magazines. In 1954, the team built two similar tracts in Anaheim—the Frematic Homes off La Palma and Brookhurst (and a nearby second phase off Gilbert and Broadway)—a couple miles northwest of the new Disneyland project. For the first time, Cortese used full-page ads to announce the openings of his phases, as well as appearances by GE spokesperson Betty Furness. The homes were even more successful than the ranchos.

Fresh off two big successes, Cortese went for the fences with his next project, Rossmoor.

While Los Alamitos leaders were embroiled in their annexation scenarios to the east, equally dramatic events were happening to the south and west. On August 19, 1955, the *Enterprise* reported that "rumors are hot on 7,000 homes in Los Alamitos." Chamber of commerce leaders said a builder, later revealed to be Ross Cortese, had control of almost 1,500 acres and definitely would subdivide it, including a 50-acre shopping center. They wanted the land to be in a city. If Los Alamitos wouldn't incorporate, then Buena Park was an option.

This heightened the battle for annexation and incorporation that led to the incorporation of Cypress, as detailed in the previous chapter.

During all this, Cortese worked with the state and county to establish a water district and get an exact location of the freeway finally established. The State Highway Commission's final plan had the freeways taking out over half of Cortese's proposed development, but nonetheless, in May 1956, the *Enterprise* headline read, "Tract Land Sale Largest Ever Recorded in County":

> *The sale of a total of 756 acres of subdivision land south of Katella and west of Los Alamitos Blvd. was named by Orange County officials as the largest ever recorded in Orange County.*
>
> *Sold by the Irvine Company, Mr. and Mrs. W.B. Hellis and W.S. Tuback (which purchased the land from the Susanna Bixby Bryant Estate in 1947), the buyers reportedly included California Gov. Goodwin Knight, Alfred Gitelson, Morris Kawin, and Edward Rothschild, who are listed as the Lakewood Rancho Land Company. Developer of the subdivision is Ross Cortese, who built the Lakewood Rancho Estates and the Frematic Homes in Anaheim.*
>
> *A total of 2,398 homes is scheduled for the area, with three elementary schools proposed as well as two big shopping centers. One is to be 14 acres at Katella and Los Alamitos Blvd, and the other 17 acres further south on the boulevard.*
>
> *Typical lots in the subdivision show 7,210 square feet on 70 by 102 foot lots. School sites shown are 10, 9.1, and 9.8 acres.*
>
> *The tract is tentatively named "Rossmor" [sic] and is scheduled to come before the planning commission June 6. Time tables call for the major share of the development within two years.*

A Brief History of Los Alamitos and Rossmoor

Cortese's envisioned community was actually made of three separate parcels. The northernmost section (above Orangewood) originally belonged to the Bixby Land Company but had been farmed by the DeCramers for a number of years. The middle section between Orangewood and Main Way was the Susanna Bixby Bryant land, which was sold after her death in 1947 to the Irvine-Tubeck-Hellis group. It was these two sections that Cortese first secured rights to, but he apparently also had an option in place with the Fred Bixby Ranch Company for the southern half of the tract, south of Bixby Road (now Main Way). When that was completed, the number of homes would eventually reach over 3,200—an incredible number for a time when most developers built tracts of less than 300 homes. (Lakewood was the most notable exception.)

Interestingly, Cortese's acquisition of the northernmost section of his Rossmoor development included the land where Oak Middle School and Los Alamitos City Hall now stand, as well as the parcel now occupied by St. Hedwig and Good Shepherd Churches and the Rossmoor Highlands.

With Rossmoor, Cortese elevated himself to a whole new level of builder-merchant, and the marketing for his new community went to a whole new level as well.

Where Lakewood and Los Altos were mostly aimed at first-time homebuyers, Rossmoor was targeted at successful professionals ready to expand their families. The lots were bigger and the streets wider, and instead of a plain grid of streets, Cortese employed the garden city designs using curving roads with T-stops and streets that would end at one block and start up again a few blocks over. While this perplexed some drivers, studies showed that it funneled traffic to main arteries and led to fewer accidents.

The brochures labeled Rossmoor as "Long Beach's smartest new suburb." And as he had with the Lakewood Rancho Estates, Cortese utilized top creative talent to make those brochures, in this case artist Robert Perine, who would gain fame later that year for his marketing campaign that would make Fender Guitar a worldwide name.

Cliff May and Chris Choate were not the original architects for Rossmoor. After their Anaheim Frematic partnership, May especially had

Ross Cortese and Rossmoor

The brochures for Rossmoor borrowed much from the simplicity of Perine's Ranchos work. The original Rossmoor sales brochure (above) used a signature phrase "Long Beach's smartest new suburb." The back page highlighted the proximity of the new Long Beach State University and noted that the "distinguished institution with a brilliant future" would "help Rossmoor follow in the tradition of Berkeley and Westwood." The college connection was reemphasized in the names of the tract's early phases: the Cornell, the Yale, et cetera.

some differences with Cortese, but he was also involved at the time in his Sun Estates development in Anaheim. Choate however, would come back to design Rossmoor's award-winning Estates phase in 1959. But for his original Rossmoor architect, Cortese went to another "hot" name. Earl Kaltenbach, Jr. had just designed the recently opened Tomorrowland at Disneyland. For Rossmoor, Kaltenbach utilized gingerbread trim with bird's nests but obviously borrowed much of May and Choate's ranch floor plans—post-and-beam sections, floor-to-ceiling glass doors and windows and L-shaped layouts with pitched overhanging roofs. (Maybe it was these borrowings that peeved May so much.) Kaltenbach himself described the homes as an "integrated design" utilizing "features borrowed from the past and incorporated with the latest in modern planning and design."

A Brief History of Los Alamitos and Rossmoor

Cortese often used television to promote Rossmoor. The tract's development and construction were featured on *The Atlantic Richfield Hour* in early 1957, and in 1959, Cortese again brought attention to the tract by giving away a home on *Queen for a Day*. The winner was Shirley Woodlock, a twenty-eight-year-old Downey woman who is shown at left with *Queen for a Day* host Jack Bailey. Separated from her husband, she said she originally went on the show to get a garage partition so she could set up a small nursery to produce income to support her family.

Ross Cortese and Rossmoor

Cortese's marketing machine went into full gear in late 1956, releasing a blizzard of newspaper articles beginning before the model homes opened on Rossmoor Way. The campaign included full-page ads (sometimes two full pages) in every Sunday's *LA Times*, articles extolling Rossmoor's modern construction and equally all-American virtues. Be it all-electric kitchens, an appearance by GE spokeswoman Betty Furness, the Christmas decorations parade winners, the new Little League, the very active women's club, the opening of new schools and new stores, the new shopping center and the latest sold-out phase, it was all chronicled and hyped by Cortese's publicists. And for it, Cortese and his marketing team would be honored by his developer/homebuilder peers and marketing associations.

Originally, the marketers emphasized the proximity to Long Beach State. Ads touted Rossmoor as "in the tradition of Westwood and Berkeley." The first two phases were the Yale and Princeton. Even before the first homeowners moved in, those two phases were sold out, and the builders announced a third phase, the Cornell. Apparently, once the freeway began construction, the college connection was forgotten.

Cortese even started his own newspaper, the *Rossmoor News* (the first four-page issue was available in December 1956 to visitors who viewed the new model homes). As Cortese humbly noted in his page-one column, "It's the first time in history a newspaper has been published in a town without any people in it!"

Issue three (April 1957) had pictures of soon-to-be residents, including Long Beach banker Art Frenzel and his charming wife, Betty; Army lieutenant colonel M.C. Quillen; Frank and Betty Lott and their daughters, Carol and Marilynn (Frank was manager of Foster & Kleiser Outdoor Advertising); and Hal Shideler, general manager of Long Beach radio station KFOX. These vignettes, and thirteen others in the issue, not only let homeowners meet their new neighbors but also let potential buyers know the quality of people in the neighborhood. Elitist? Perhaps. Effective? Definitely.

The June 6, 1957 *Enterprise* reported that Rossmoor's first residents—Mr. and Mrs. Sam J. Musser—had moved into their new home at 3182 Kempton Drive. He was a retired sales manager for the Armour Meat Packing

A Brief History of Los Alamitos and Rossmoor

Company plant in St. Joseph, Missouri. The Mussers didn't have school-age children, but they were a rarity. Los Alamitos school superintendent Jack L. Weaver—who oversaw 600 total students attending schools with a capacity of 300—was expecting 150 new students a week as a result of the new families moving into Rossmoor.

Within four years, there would be almost fourteen thousand people in Rossmoor. In the 1960 census, its population surpassed Los Alamitos, Seal Beach and Cypress combined.

It had numbers, it had vitality and it had opinions, but it rarely had unity—at least when it came to incorporation. In its first five years of existence, it tried to incorporate three different times. It failed each time.

The professors, lawyers and public officials among them tried to get the community incorporated. But many who had run their own companies and had experienced city governments forcing intrusive, unwanted restrictions on them wanted nothing to do with another government to answer to. So Rossmoor remained unincorporated. It was too big for Los Alamitos to absorb in a hostile takeover. But it wasn't big enough—or organized enough—to stop a determined property owner, an ambitious city and an unconcerned county to prevent Seal Beach from acquiring its main areas of retail revenue. But that story is for another time.

The success of Rossmoor drastically changed Cortese's life. "We were doing well," remembers Heidi, "but all of a sudden things got…nicer." Professionally, Cortese moved into the top tier of developer-homebuilders. His methods for developing and marketing large communities were adopted by builders all over Southern California and the nation. But he was not one to rest on his laurels. Seeing how many older retired homebuyers—like the Mussers—considered his Rossmoor community, he began to focus on that growing demographic, developing the concept he eventually marketed as "retirement living" through his first Leisure World development. It was a market that had actually been first tried on a small scale as an Israeli kibbutz and then in Florida (again on a smaller scale). Now Cortese was doing it big, as was Del Webb, who was simultaneously building his Sun City community outside Phoenix, Arizona. As the owner of the New York Yankees and the builder of the Sahara Hotel-Casino in

Ross Cortese and Rossmoor

Las Vegas, Webb got the most publicity. But it was Cortese who was the most innovative.

Some doubters called it a geriatric ghetto, but when the first of 6,500 Leisure World units in Seal Beach went up for sale, qualifying homebuyers—like they had with Rossmoor—rushed to buy houses in Cortese's idea of retirement heaven.

Rossmoor had made Cortese a household name. Rossmoor Leisure World took it ten steps further, and Cortese became more associated with the latter. More importantly, future events showed that the development of Leisure World would end up choking the growth of Rossmoor while creating some for Los Alamitos.

11
CITYHOOD FOR LOS AL

As the 1950s came to an end, so had Los Alamitos's lifestyle as a small town surrounded by miles of open farmland.

Long Beach now spread to the Orange County line. The Bixby Land Company had sold what would become El Dorado Park (originally proposed as Los Alamitos Park) to the City of Long Beach in return for significant tax breaks. Just south of that, the Bixby Ranch Company was selling off or subdividing its land parcel by parcel.

One of those former parcels was now Long Beach State College, which had now become one of the state's largest universities, with student enrollment at more than ten thousand. (By 1966, that number would be twenty thousand. In 2012, its total enrollment surpassed thirty-three thousand.)

The county line at Coyote Creek protected Los Alamitos and Rossmoor from annexation attempts from that direction and from north and east of town. The new leaders of Cypress, quite happy with their dairies and the Los Alamitos Race Track, had thwarted Buena Park's expansionist designs.

But southeast of the base, Garden Grove and Westminster were still in expansion mode. Garden Grove's downtown core was almost due south of Disneyland, but it had now extended its tentacles west by annexing a five-mile-long strip of land 250 feet wide along Garden Grove Boulevard to Miller (now Valley View). They were in an annexation race with

Cityhood for Los Al

Westminster, which momentarily stalled the Garden Grove growth by attempting to annex a square mile north of Garden Grove Boulevard, overlapping Garden Grove's planned annexation. The Los Alamitos leaders (i.e., the chamber of commerce and the school district) knew that there was still a distinct possibility of being gobbled up by either Garden Grove or Westminster or ending up totally isolated if either city followed through on its threats to annex the air station and the two proposed shopping centers, Thriftimart (now Von's) at Los Al and Farquhar and the Rossmoor Center. If any of these annexations happened, Los Alamitos would be left as an island on the edge of the county, with no future of cityhood—the only alternative probably being to annex to Westminster.

In March 1959, some Los Al leaders, including Bill Brown, the new president of the chamber of commerce, working with Rossmoor leaders like Arthur Miller, put forth another incorporation try whose boundaries were roughly present-day Los Alamitos, Rossmoor, College Parks East and West and that part of present Garden Grove north of the Garden Grove Freeway and west of Valley View/Bolsa Chica. It would be ten square miles. But the petitions—which required the written consent of the owners of 25 percent of the land valuation and 25 percent of the area residents—couldn't get enough signatures.

The situation became more urgent when Garden Grove and Westminster reached an accord in May 1959. Westminster would stop its expansion at Garden Grove Boulevard. Garden Grove was free to push on to the county line, try to annex the base and grab the grand prize—the tax dollars that would be generated by the then-under-construction Rossmoor Shopping Center.

Complicating matters was a July 1959 campaign to "relocate the Los Al Naval Air Station," led by a group of Westminster and Garden Grove developers and union leaders representing building trades. Only one "local" was involved in the campaign. Dairyman Ale Tuinhout, who owned much of the property south of the Navy Golf Course, had optioned it to a developer, and now both indicated they felt the base should be moved, which would allow for more residential development, mainly allowing schools to be constructed in the area. Schools were prohibited for being too close to the flight path.

A Brief History of Los Alamitos and Rossmoor

Los Alamitos residents fumed at these "outsiders." Lura Labourdette, the chamber secretary and Los Alamitos resident for thirty-five years, pointed out that most of the rentals in Los Alamitos were occupied by Naval personnel, and many families had owned homes here for eight or nine years. In civic activities, Naval personnel had leaned over backward to cooperate with the townspeople.

Fortunately, that "Oust the Navy" effort fizzled, as the navy didn't want to go anywhere at that time, and it usually got what it wanted.

In late July 1959, Los Al Chamber of Commerce leaders began circulating another incorporation petition, this time excluding most of Rossmoor, except for the northern, mostly unoccupied part above Orangewood and the Rossmoor Shopping Center. Even before it was formerly announced, the Rossmoor Homeowners Association voted thirty-four to two in opposition to these boundaries, saying it would severely damage any future Rossmoor incorporation attempts.

Things heated up even more at a Rossmoor homeowners meeting held on Monday, September 14, 1959, at Rossmoor School. A discussion of incorporation pros and cons deteriorated into a "series of accusations and threats against the Chamber of Commerce and the merchants of Los Alamitos." One Rossmoor resident called for boycotts against Los Alamitos merchants who were members of the chamber. "I wouldn't even use his restroom," he shouted.

When chamber president William Brown was invited up to answer questions, the *Enterprise* reporter (probably editor-publisher Dale Kroesen) wrote, "embarrassment and indignation of those present were evident" when another Rossmoor speaker said Los Alamitos looked as if "a Santa Ana wind had hit it and the town was in need of paint."

Rossmoor Homeowners Association (RHA) board member Arthur Miller criticized the attacks as "insulting and rude and for a group of supposedly intelligent people, the conduct was deplorable." The crowd responded with a long ovation. The rest of the meeting continued in a civil manner and ended with the RHA agreeing to send a letter requesting that all Rossmoor territory be removed from the petition. (At this time, Rossmoor included all the Ross Cortese–controlled property—the land where St. Hedwig and Good Shepherd Church and the Rossmoor

Highlands are now located and the land where Los Alamitos City Hall, Oak School and SuperMedia now stand, as well as the Bixby Ranch-owned "Old Ranch Town Center" and Golf Club.)

Perhaps motivated by the Rossmoor insults, 430 Los Alamitos residents signed the petition for incorporation, twice the required number of 215. But in a late drive, the RHA, Ross Cortese, the Irvine Company (owners of the Rossmoor land north of Orangewood) and the Bixby Ranch Company got the Orange County supervisors to exclude all Rossmoor area from the final proposed city boundaries. Simultaneously, these groups got their own Rossmoor incorporation attempt approved.

The Los Alamitos incorporation vote was set for February 1960. The Rossmoor vote was set for the following June.

In 1959, Oscar and Anna Watte's family moved out of their ranch and farm (just west of the present Sprouts location), which their family had occupied for fifty-one years. They would soon be moving to Tulare County, joining their children Omer and George and vacating their home for the proposed development of the Rossmoor Shopping Center.

In late 1959, the plans for the Center—a $20 million, eighty-acre grand co-venture of the Cortese partners and the Bixby Ranch Company—were approved by the board of supervisors. The area's other proposed shopping center, Builder Harry Rinker's shopping center on Los Alamitos Boulevard between Farquhar and Orangewood, was, per the *Times*, opposed by Ross Cortese, who "felt it would compete with his own center."

Behind Rinker's Center, William Lyon's Luxury Homes Company was already constructing Dutch Haven, one of many Dutch Havens tracts being built in Southern California communities, including Buena Park, Huntington Beach, Anaheim and the Conejo Valley in Ventura County. Like Cortese, Lyon would become one of the nation's top homebuilders over the next decade.

Approval of Rinker's project was stalled for four to five months, partly by opposition from Cortese, but of equal importance was the construction of a couple flood control ditches in that area. Ultimately, with strong backing from the chamber of commerce, Rinker's Center was approved in December 1959, although it was not allowed to reach

A Brief History of Los Alamitos and Rossmoor

Orangewood for two reasons. One was to provide an easement for the Flood Channel on the north side of the street. The second reason was that prior to this, Cortese wanted to place the new public junior high school at the southeast corner of Orangewood and Los Alamitos Boulevard. But federal law prohibited a public school from being constructed so close to an air base. Cortese ended up donating the land to the Roman Catholic Diocese to construct a new church, with the condition it be called St. Hedwig. The supervisors confirmed the zoning of Rinker's land just north as residential to provide a buffer between the church and shopping center. It became another entrance to the Dutch Haven tract.

Why the condition to name the church St. Hedwig? Ross's daughter Heidi says there were multiple reasons. Hedwig was not only patron saint of Poland but also the first name of Cortese's mother-in-law (Hedwig Himsl Goetten) and was also the given first name of Heidi—Hedwig Alona Cortese—who was eight years old at the time. "Both of us were called Hedy, a name I hated because I was teased about it, especially after [actress] Hedy Lamar got caught shoplifting," remembers Heidi Cortese. "But I finally got people to call me Heidi."

St. Hedwig opened in mid-May 1960 (and St. Isidore was made a satellite sub-parish). Cortese later sold the Hedwig parish the adjacent land where the baseball field and school are now located. A year later, Ross Cortese sold the land south of St. Hedwig for a new Presbyterian church, which opened in November 1961 as Good Shepherd Presbyterian Church. It would be the area's fifth church, following Bethlehem Lutheran—which held its first service on September 18, 1960, in the western room at the Los Alamitos Racetrack. Within a year, Ross Cortese would let it use the recently closed Rossmoor Homes sales offices at Rossmoor Way and Weatherby Road.

The public junior high school would be built a few years later on Cortese's land north of Katella. Ironically, it was right behind another plot of Cortese-controlled land on which was built a new Los Alamitos City Hall, which is still in use.

Cortese's original plans also called for a $3 million hospital to be constructed at the southwest corner of Katella and Los Alamitos Boulevard, but this, too, was denied by the supervisors. Undaunted,

Cortese made arrangements for it to become another shopping center: the Rossmoor Village, where Fio Rito's and the Fish Company now stand.

In early 1959 another forty-acre tract of 139 homes was announced to be located a half mile east of Lexington Drive by yet another builder, the J.T. Hintz Co. Strangely, even though it continued the custom of naming the streets after aircraft carriers (although its roads ran east–west instead of north–south), it was not included as part of Carrier Row and is the only set of homes in the area to keep its original tract name, New Dutch Haven.

With Disneyland at one end, Rossmoor at the other and the Los Alamitos Racetrack in between, Katella became one of the main east–west thoroughfares in Orange County, and certainly much busier. St. Isidore pastor Dominick Daley told the *LA Times*, "I could sit in my church office and during a day hear hardly more than a dozen cars drive along Katella Avenue. Now 25,000 cars a day roll by as our community grows." With plans underway to extend Katella into Long Beach, it would become almost twice as busy.

Although Cortese encountered setbacks, he was busier than ever. He and Alona bought a large section of land in Huntington Beach. In early 1960, he finalized the purchase of a large parcel from the Hellman Ranch and was just getting started with the development of Leisure World, the shopping center was under construction and new phases kept opening for Rossmoor.

The Los Alamitos–Rossmoor area was the second-fastest-growing area in Orange County, behind only Anaheim. The tax revenue of the new shopping centers was still very inviting. But as Rossmoor and other tracts surrounded the base, it seemed inevitable to all that the military base had to be closed, making an additional 1,300 acres available for development.

Thus, amidst the background of all this proposed and assumed growth, and with the threat of annexation by Garden Grove looming even larger, on February 24, 1960, Los Alamitos residents went to the polls to decide their future. The proposed town had a population of nearly 3,000, with 987 registered to vote. By a vote of 379 for and 251 opposed, the community became Orange County's twenty-second city.

A BRIEF HISTORY OF LOS ALAMITOS AND ROSSMOOR

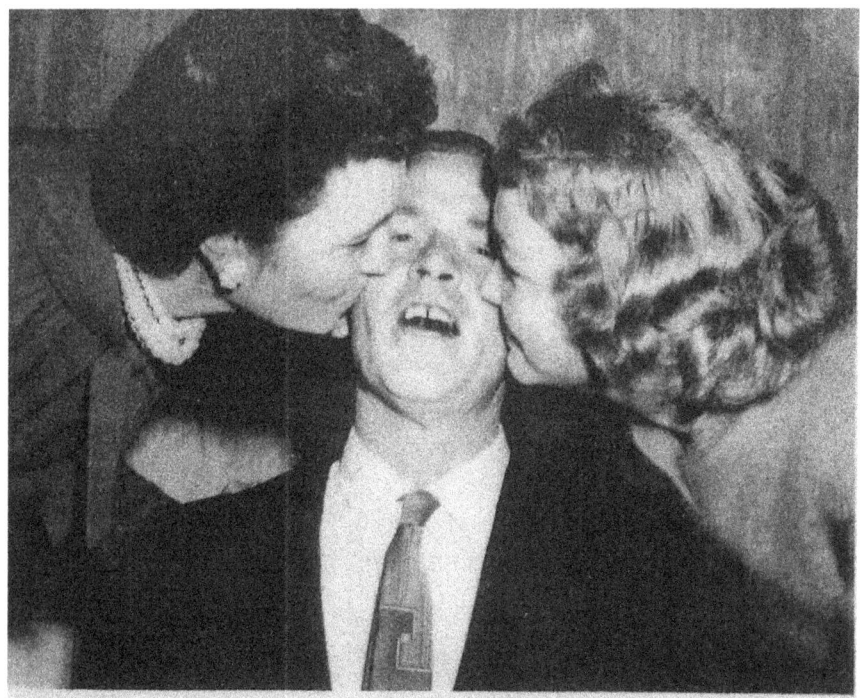

Bell First Mayor Of Los Alamitos

LONG-TIME CIVILIAN EMPLOYEE James V. Bell gets a happy sendoff on his career as the first Mayor of the new City of Los Alamitos from his wife, left, and daughter, Sylvia, 16. Los Alamitos officially became Orange County's 22nd city after a hard-fought incorporation movement. Mayor Bell will continue his duties in the LosAl electric shop.

Photo Courtesy of the Santa Ana Register

Chamber of commerce leader Jim Bell received two kisses to celebrate two victories in February 1960, when Los Alamitos voters not only approved incorporation as Orange County's twenty-second city but also gave him the most votes from the community. He would become the town's first mayor. The night was the culmination of seven years of hard work for Bell and other Los Alamitos area leaders.

To run the new town, the residents also voted in some familiar faces. Leading in the voting for the new city council was James V. Bell, the man who had led the charge to reinvigorate the sleepy town some thirteen years before. He received 401 votes, followed by Chuck Long (398), Bill Brown (364), Frank Allen (359) and A.C. Brown (344).

Four months later, Rossmoor's attempt to incorporate failed by a vote of 1,615 to 1,315.

Cityhood for Los Al

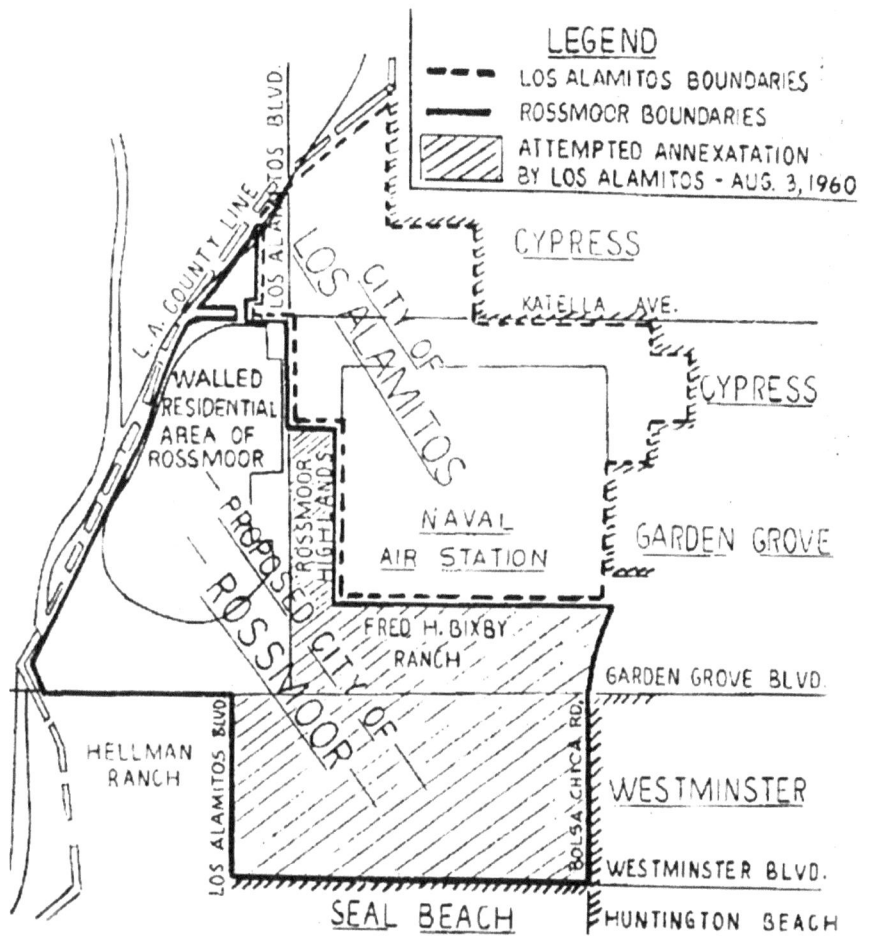

The *Press-Telegram* asked if this was the "City of Tomorrow" in June 1960, when Rossmoor residents made their most serious attempt at incorporation. The boundaries included significant parts of present Los Alamitos (the Rossmoor Highlands, Oak Middle School and the Los Al City Hall Offices), Seal Beach (all of the Old Ranch Center and Golf Course, the Rossmoor Center, College Park East and most of the Naval Weapons Station) and much of Garden Grove. When the vote failed, Los Alamitos leaders immediately moved in to annex that area surrounding Rossmoor proper that wasn't controlled by the Fred Bixby Ranch Company or the Hellman Ranch.

From here on in, the story gets even more interesting. But that, too, is for another time.

EPILOGUE

The year 1960 signaled the beginning of an era and the end of another.

In January 1960, Henry Lucas, the sugar company's second-longest employee, died in Los Alamitos at the age of eighty-three. After the company moved operations to Santa Ana, Lucas acted as the old factory's caretaker until it was sold. He still stayed on as caretaker for the new owners.

In November 1960, Gus Strodthoff, the sugar company's longest-tenured employee, died. He had started as an office boy, and in 1898, as a secretary to J. Ross Clark, he cut the check for the purchase of the eight thousand acres of land that became the Montana Ranch. Strodthoff advanced to be plant superintendent, and as the final president of the Montana Land Company, he signed the documents dissolving the company and selling many of its assets to the Holly Sugar Company and the land to the builders of Lakewood. Strodthoff lived his final years in a home on Ocean Avenue in Seal Beach.

In late 1959, Orange County officials declared the old sugar factory building dangerous and a public nuisance. Not wanting to spend the money on upgrades, the property owners hired a demolitions expert to bring down the old factory.

For fifty-four years, the Los Alamitos sugar factory had been the local landmark. Built by some of the most wealthy and powerful men

Epilogue

FAREWELL, SWEET MEMORIES

Wreckers Nibble Away Sugar Mill

WRECKERS HAVE REDUCED old sugar factory at Los Alamitos to a skeleton. The big smokestack, featured in photo at right showing the buildings before demolition began, will linger two weeks as a passing monument to the mill's former glory. (Staff)

With the incorporation of Los Alamitos, 1960 marked a new era for the Los Alamitos–Rossmoor area, but it also symbolized the end of the past with the dismantling of the main buildings of the old sugar factory. It didn't go easy, as the old smokestacks, which had been an area landmark for over sixty years, withstood the first few attempts at dynamite before finally falling in December 1960.

in America, it ushered in a new era for Orange County, an era when sugar beets were the dominant crop in the area. After its sugar operations were moved, it housed pet food and served as a warehouse for thousands of bales of cotton and for products manufactured by Douglas Aircraft. The old garage and machine shop was still used as a lumber mill, the cottages still housed residents and several other small businesses used smaller buildings.

Demolition of the main factory building began in June 1960. By July 4, only the tall smokestacks remained. The demolition company said the stacks would be down within two weeks.

The factory had other ideas. In October, before a crowd of onlookers, the demo charges once again failed to bring down the smokestacks.

Local history, it seems, did not want to go away that easily.

SOURCES

Good starting points for any study of the history of the Los Alamitos–Rossmoor area are the many articles by local historian (and my friend and neighbor) Margret Kendrick. Her help, and the help of many others with the Los Alamitos Museum (especially Marilynn Poe and Leon Sjostrom) have been extremely valuable.

The Rancho Los Alamitos staff has been immensely helpful in providing me with maps, court documents and extensive information, and I'd like to especially thank executive director Pamela Seagar for making so much of their information available to me.

The Rancho Los Cerritos Library is also a good resource, although its sources primarily focus on the Long Beach activities of the Lewellyn and Jotham Bixby lines and are shy much information on the Bixby Land Company's Alamitos lands.

I have used far too many sources to list here, but some of the best ones are:

Chapter 1

Gumprecht, Blake. *The Los Angeles River: Its Life, Death, and Possible Rebirth (Creating the North American Landscape.* Baltimore, MD, Johns Hopkins University Press, 1999.

SOURCES

Rivers and Mountains Conservancy publications.
Stein, Eric D. *Historical Ecology of the Southern California wetlands*, Southern California Coastal Waters Research Project. Technical Report, 2007.
U.S. Geological Survey. Numerous reports on the San Gabriel Mountains and River and wetlands.

There are many sources on the local Native American culture. Beyond numerous books, local government Environmental Impact Reports (EIRs) are great starting points, although not always totally accurate. There is a good healthy academic controversy going on about the extent and impact of Tongva culture in this area, not only between Native American activists but also between professors like Matthew A. Boxt and Mark Raab at UC Santa Barbara and Long Beach State.

CHAPTER 2

Cleland, Robert Glass. *Cattle on a Thousand Hills*. San Marino, CA: Huntington Library/Ward Ritchie Press, 1951. [This is an excellent book on the Spanish and Mexican era and on the Abel Stearns story. Cleland, a history professor at Occidental College, also provides valuable information in his books on I.W. Hellman and the Irvine Ranch.]

CHAPTERS 3 AND 4

Bixby Smith, Sarah. *Adobe Days*. Lincoln: University of Nebraska Press, 1987.
Dinkelspiel, Frances. *Towers of Gold: How One Jewish Immigrant Named Isais Hellman Created California*. New York: St. Martins Press, 2008. [This biography of the author's great-grandfather I.W. Hellman is thin on Alamitos-related details, but her thorough reporting on the Huntington-Hellman relationship led me to Hellman's correspondence at the California Historical Society, where I discovered much Alamitos-related correspondence between

Sources

Hellman and the likes of Philip A. Stanton, the Bixbys, *LA Times* owner Harrison G. Otis and others.]

Flint, Thomas. *Diary of Dr. Thomas Flint. California to Maine and Return, 1851–1855*. Claremont, CA, 1924.

Lavender, David. *Historical Narrative: Rancho Los Alamitos*. Long Beach, CA: Rancho Los Alamitos Foundation, n.d. [The text is heavily utilized and expanded in *Rancho Los Alamitos: Ever Changing, Always the Same* (Claudia K. Jurmain, with David Lavender and Larry L. Meyer, Berkely, CA: Heyday Books, 2011), which, although its primary focus is on the John W. and Fred Bixby family and the family's Long Beach property, is another excellent resource.]

Woodbridge, Sarah. *Rancho Los Alamitos: Architectural Historical Narrative*. Long Beach, CA: Rancho Los Alamitos Foundation, n.d. [Original research by Loretta Berner and Pamela Young.]

Chapter 5

Invaluable resources on the sugar beet days (Los Alamitos from 1896 through 1925) are the old issues of the *Los Angeles Times*, the *Anaheim Bulletin* and the *Santa Ana* [now Orange County] *Register*. Equally indispensable are the various sugar beet industry publications—*Sugar, The Louisiana Sugar Planter*, et cetera—which have only recently become available to all through the digitization efforts of Google Books. In recent years, even more original source items have been made available through the Online Archive of California and the Library of Congress.

Chapters 6 and 7

In addition to many newspaper articles, the first-person memoirs of early Los Alamitos residents Harry and Nellie Butterfield and Joseph Denni (all children in turn-of-the-century Los Alamitos) and Bessie Juskievicz and Lura Green Labourdette provide a great insight into the young town of Los Alamitos in its first fifty years. They are available at the Los

Alamitos Museum, as are many later-in-life newspaper interviews with other longtime residents. Information on Belgians around Los Alamitos comes from Fred V. Goeman's *Belgian Immigrants in California*. (Belgium: self-published, 1998). Useful for double-checking are the 1900, 1910, 1920, 1930 and 1940 U.S. censuses, as well as the many Orange County directories published annually.

CHAPTER 8

Los Alamitos Air Base history during its Navy phase is a real challenge. Many early Navy photos and records of NAS Los Alamitos were reportedly removed or destroyed when the Navy departed in the early 1970s. Fortunately, there are many newspaper articles and numerous first-person accounts of navy pilots' brief experiences at NAS Los Alamitos during World War II and the Korean conflicts. The two best are *Skipper: Confessions of a Fighter Squadron Commander* (Mesa, AZ: Champlin Fighter Museum Press, 1985) by Hugh Winters, the commander of Fighting 19 and later all of Air Group 19, and the privately circulated *Voices of Bomber 19*, which collated all the memories of those Bomber Group 19 pilots and radiomen/gunners who were still alive in the late 1980s. This was done by Bill Emerson.

Other military memoirs with good sections on Los Al are *Wings and Warriors* (Washington, D.C.: Smithsonian Institution Press, 1997) by Admiral Donald D. Engen (former commander in chief of the Atlantic Fleet and former director of the Smithsonian's National Air and Space Museum) and *Sinking the Rising Sun: Dive Bombing and Dog Fighting in World War II* (St. Paul, MN: Zenith Press, 2007) by William E. Davis. Although the latter is very colorful, his version doesn't always mesh with the timelines of others.

SOURCES

Chapter 9

Most information on Los Alamitos Racetrack owner Frank Vessels was obtained from articles in the *Los Angeles Times*, the *Press-Telegram* and, to a lesser extent, the *Enterprise* (now the *News-Enterprise*) and through conversations and correspondence with Marv Haney, a horseman himself and whose father, Howell "Hal" Haney, was one of Vessel's best friends and an original and longtime member of the Los Al Race Course Board of Directors. As a high school student, Marv himself worked for Vessels on the very first Sunday "betless" horse races.

Chapter 10

Information on Ross Cortese was obtained from numerous sources, mainly articles in the *LA Times*, the *Press-Telegram, Time* magazine and published interviews with Cortese, May and Choate, as well as the other architects and businessmen he dealt with, including Pres Hotchkis Jr. of the Bixby Ranch on Company. My thanks to Heidi Cortese, who filled in many gaps and questions during our long phone conversation. My thanks also to the late Teri Messersmith, who had firsthand involvement with Cortese as an original Rossmoor homeowner and the first secretary of the Rossmoor Little League.

Chapter 11

The events leading up to cityhood are well documented in the *Times, Press-Telegram* and *Enterprise*. I have also interviewed many local old-timers in an effort to get as many viewpoints as possible.

I know that some, after reading this, might say, "That's not how it happened." To that I can only say, "Write your own book."

Sources

Hopefully, by then, there will be even more old photos, letters or other documents to help researchers. I have already tried to put much of these documents online at my www.losalhistory.com site, which hopefully will allow others to study it, add to it or analyze it—perhaps better than me.

We have a pretty interesting history. Why keep it to ourselves?

ABOUT THE AUTHOR

Larry Strawther has been writing professionally since high school—for newspapers, musical comedy groups, television, movies and now books.

He has been a writer, script consultant and executive producer for the television classics *Happy Days*, *Laverne & Shirley* and *Night Court* and the co-creator and executive producer of the cult comedy hit *MXC (Most Extreme Elimination Challenge)*.

But he has also written for movies (*Without a Clue*, a Sherlock Holmes comedy), game shows (head writer on *Jeopardy!* in 1978–79) and for comedians such as Bob Hope, Rich Little and others and has even been a Bay Area sportswriter (late 1960s–early 1970s).

Somehow he also found time to be a writer-performer for the San Francisco comedy band Butch Whacks & the Glass Packs, full time from 1973 to 1976 (opening for the Doobie Brothers, Tower of Power and Ike and Tina Turner, among others), and since 1983 has done a once-a-year annual "farewell performance," which sells out a weekend set every June.

He is also a history buff and has written numerous local history articles for local publications, runs a local history website and can now officially say he has written a history book.

Visit us at
www.historypress.net

www.ingramcontent.com/pod-product-compliance
Lightning Source LLC
Chambersburg PA
CBHW060801100426
42813CB00004B/906